100

THINGS TO DO IN
TUCSON
BEFORE YOU
DIE

D1570335

100

THINGS TO DO IN
TUCSON
BEFORE YOU
DIE

• •

CLARK NORTON

REEDY PRESS

Copyright © 2017 by Reedy Press, LLC
Reedy Press
PO Box 5131
St. Louis, MO 63139 USA
www.reedypress.com

No part of this publication may be reproduced or transmitted in any form or by any means, electronic or mechanical, including photocopy, recording, or any information storage and retrieval system, without permission in writing from the publisher.

Permissions may be sought directly from Reedy Press at the above mailing address or via our website at www.reedypress.com.

Library of Congress Control Number: 2017934538

ISBN: 9781681061009

Design by Jill Halpin

All photos courtesy of Visit Tucson.

Printed in the United States of America
17 18 19 20 21 22   5 4 3 2

Please note that websites, phone numbers, addresses, and company names are subject to change or cancellation. We did our best to relay the most accurate information available, but due to circumstances beyond our control, please do not hold us liable for misinformation. When exploring new destinations, please do your homework before you go.

DEDICATION

The author dedicates this book to young Conrad Norton,
toddler-about-town and our family's first native Tucsonan,
and to his ever-attentive parents, Grael and Nona, who make sure
he doesn't toddle too close to the cacti.

• •

CONTENTS

• •

Music and Entertainment

• •

Sports and Recreation

• •

Culture and History

• •

Shopping and Fashion

ACKNOWLEDGMENTS

I would like to thank the following people for their valuable assistance on *100 Things to Do in Tucson Before You Die:* Dan Gibson, Brad and Maria Lawrence, Jennifer Allen, Gentry Spronken, Kelly Wiehe, Justin Germain, Roland Sarlot, Susan Eyed, Margaret Shirer, Genia Parker, Todd Sadow, Margaret Feinman, Howard and Diana Kohn, Michael and Mary Reiter, Mary Beth Norton, Michael Livermore, Lia Norton—and special thanks to Barbara Northcott, Josh Stevens, Lanna Demers, and Don Korte at Reedy Press for giving me the opportunity to write this book; to Grael Norton and Nona Patrick, who first introduced me to Tucson and continue to advise me on all their favorite things to do here; and to my wife, Catharine Norton, who has accompanied me throughout my research, made indispensable suggestions on the manuscript, and truly made this book possible.

—Clark Norton, Tucson, Arizona

PREFACE

In *100 Things to Do in Tucson Before You Die,* you'll find a number of recurring themes: life in the desert, the history of the Old West, the influences of Spain and nearby Mexico (which at one time both claimed this region), the pulsating culinary and arts scenes, the rebirth of downtown Tucson, the many contributions of the University of Arizona to the intellectual and cultural life of the city, as well as the remarkable range of recreational opportunities here: hiking, biking, horseback riding, golfing, ballooning—and rooting for the Arizona Wildcats.

Compared to much of the United States, Tucson's climate turns the calendar on its head: winter, not summer, is when most events take place. The "season" for outdoor and even many indoor activities runs roughly from September or October until April or May, before the searing summer heat (up to 115 degrees Fahrenheit!) sends most everyone scurrying indoors or to cooler climes. Some attractions shorten their hours or close down altogether from June to August. Those Tucsonans who brave summer in the Old Pueblo, as the city is known, enjoy uncrowded roads, plenty of seating at their favorite restaurants (at least the ones that remain open), the welcome respite of drenching monsoon rains, and bragging rights to being true desert denizens—even if they have their central AC to thank.

Tucson's 550,000 residents (and a million in the metropolitan area) have much to be proud of. Tucson was recently named the country's first "World City of Gastronomy" by UNESCO, in recognition of its longtime native culinary heritage, sustainable agriculture, and thriving food scene. Its downtown—once nearly deserted at night and on weekends—is now buzzing with new hotels and residential apartments, cutting-edge restaurants and bars, sold-out concerts, and festivals of every description.

But Tucson has always been known for its independence of thought and action, its love and respect for the desert environment, its frontier heritage, and its cultural diversity. The city somehow manages to absorb what would seem to be contradictory elements—rodeo riders and Rhodes scholars, stately saguaros bordering busy boulevards, the young and hip mingling with graying retirees—and successfully meld them all into a vibrant whole. (The retirees, it must be noted, can be pretty hip themselves.)

As I've discovered, there are far more than 100 things to do in Tucson, but in the book you'll find an intriguing mix of well-known attractions and off-the-beaten-path gems that even many residents may not be aware of—or have never gotten around to trying. To that end, *100 Things to Do in Tucson Before You Die* is intended to appeal to residents as well as visitors—including the many hybrid "snowbirds" who flock down from the frozen north to spend their winters here in sunshine and seventy degree weather.

Whether it's a secluded hiking trail in the nearby mountains or the frenetic action of a 100-mile bike race, a place to sip local craft beers or sample the messy delights of a Sonoran hot dog,

• •

a visit to a museum of miniatures or the country's largest gem show, a ticket to the county fair or the symphony orchestra, you'll find the whys, the wheres, and the hows within these pages — and much more. So, welcome to a Tucson that may surprise you—and will almost certainly charm you—as you explore the Old Pueblo, whether for a weekend or a lifetime.

• •

FOOD AND DRINK

DINE IN STYLE
AT DOWNTOWN KITCHEN + COCKTAILS

When James Beard Award–winning chef Janos Wilder opened his airy and inviting Downtown Kitchen + Cocktails in 2010, downtown Tucson wasn't the trendy draw it is today. Wilder, in fact, played a key role in pioneering the central city's dramatic renaissance—simply by taking a chance on the location.

But the Santa Fe– and French-trained chef has always been ahead of his time. Long before "farm to table" became a foodie mantra, Wilder's signature cooking style relied on locally sourced ingredients to assure freshness and authenticity. The seasonally changing menus may pair Southwestern style chiles with rib eye steaks or calamari, flavor cocktails with cactus syrup—or simply bring the best of the day's produce and meats from local farms and ranches direct to your plate.

135 S. 6th Avenue
520-623-7700
downtownkitchen.com

TIP

Watch for special three-course global tasting menus changing monthly June to August—a reward for staying in Tucson in the summer heat.

BINGE ON CHIMICHANGAS
AT EL CHARRO

El Charro Café—the oldest continually operated family-owned Mexican restaurant in the country, dating from 1922—is also Tucson's best-known restaurant. Often filled to capacity with overflow crowds waiting outside, El Charro is housed in a historic Presidio District building that harbors an array of rooms and courtyards. Once seated, you can sip a margarita while trying to decide among the almost dizzying selection of Sonoran Mexican standards.

The huge *carne seca* platter—beef dried in the sun on the restaurant's roof, then shredded and grilled with chile, tomato, and onion and served with guacamole, rice, and beans—is a signature dish. Another is chimichangas, deep-fried guilty pleasures invented by El Charro's founder years ago when she accidentally dropped a burrito into frying oil—and made Mexican culinary history.

311 N. Court Avenue
520-622-1922
elcharrocafe.com

TIP
Two much newer El Charro branches are located north of downtown at 6910 E. Sunrise Drive (520-514-1922) and 7725 N. Oracle Road in Oro Valley (520-229-1922)

EAT AND GREET
AT TUCSON MEET YOURSELF

In 2015, when Tucson became the first American city to be honored by UNESCO as a World City of Gastronomy, the annual Tucson Meet Yourself festival helped illustrate why. This longtime folklife and food-filled event, held over a three-day weekend downtown each fall, is rooted in the concept that Tucson's gastronomy is intertwined with its history, culture, and surroundings.

Along with music, dance, handicraft, and cooking demonstrations, dozens of food trucks serving up ethnic specialties attract throngs of festival-goers. From Persian lamb and Peruvian *lomo saltado* to Jamaican jerk chicken and Filipino noodles, authentic foods from around the globe have added immeasurable depth and flavor to the city's gastronomic stew. Tucson Meet Yourself is more than just a food fest: it's a folk cultural experience—and a very tasty one indeed.

tucsonmeetyourself.org

TAP INTO THE CRAFT BREWING CRAZE
AT BORDERLANDS

Tucson's craft beer scene is hopping, with new breweries opening every year. At least twenty brewery-based taprooms now welcome beer lovers eager to sample the latest handcrafted creations.

Borderlands Brewing Co., which opened in 2011 in a historic 1890's-era warehouse downtown, has helped set the pace. Priding itself on its Southwestern style, Borderlands turns to regionally grown ingredients—including cactus fruit juice in its Prickly Pear Wheat, roasted pecans in its Nut Brown Ale, and vanilla in its Vanilla Porter—to provide their brews with a local personality.

Borderlands is also a lively and fun place for tastings—especially in its outdoor beer garden, which comes complete with a bocce court, live music several nights a week, and other events.

119 E. Toole Street
520-261-8773
borderlandsbrewing.com

TIP
During the annual mid-February Tucson Craft Beer Crawl, you can sample beers from up to thirty brewers at nine venues in downtown Tucson. tucsoncraftbeercrawl.com

---

Here are other top craft breweries to try, including one of the signature beers for each:

1912 Brewing Co. (Mescalero Dominicano Stout)
2045 N. Forbes Boulevard, 520-256-4851,
1912brewing.com

Barrio Brewing Co. (Barrio Blonde)
800 E. 16th Street, 520-791-2739, barriobrewing.co

Dragoon Brewing Co. (Dragoon IPA)
1859 W. Grant Road, 520-329-3606,
dragoonbrewing.com

Iron John's Brewing Co. (Old Pueblo Pale Ale)
245 S. Plumer Avenue, 520-775-1727,
ironjohnsbrewing.com

Nimbus Brewery (Old Monkey Shine)
3850 E. 44th Street, 520-745-9175, nimbusbeer.com

Sentinel Peak Brewing Co. (Solida del Sol Amber)
4746 E. Grant Road, 520-777-9456,
sentinelpeakbrewing.com

Ten Fifty-Five Brewing (Sugar Skull Stout)
3810 E. 44th Street, 520-461-8073, 1055brewing.com

GRAB A BOOTH
AT THE WELCOME DINER

It's not easy replacing a beloved longtime institution, but the Welcome Diner has done just that—with style. When Chaffin's, an authentic 1950s-era diner, closed in late 2015, devotees were bereft. A year later, after a renovation that left the restaurant's distinctive mid-century modern footprint intact but spiffed up the décor, the newly opened Welcome Diner started packing in the crowds from morning till after midnight.

Hipper and more upscale than Chaffin's, but still homey, the Welcome Diner puts Southern and Southwestern twists on the menu, with specialties such as fried chicken with mashed potatoes, fried green tomato sandwich, and a jackfruit po'boy (tastes like pork!). Ingredients are locally sourced, the wait staff eager to please, and the cooking refined. Chaffin's will be missed—but its successor is more than welcome.

902 E. Broadway Boulevard
520-622-5100
welcomediner.net/broadway

TIP
The diner stays open till 2 a.m. and reopens at 9 a.m. daily.

SAMPLE MEXICO'S
DIVERSE CUISINE

Of the "best 23 miles of Mexican food" that the city visitors bureau claims for Tucson, it's safe to say that at least twenty miles represent the dishes that most Americans—and Tucsonans— know best and adore: tacos, burritos, enchiladas, tostadas, tamales, and the like. But those don't begin to encompass all that Mexican cuisine has to offer. To sample more diverse tastes of Mexico, try these stylish downtown restaurants:

At **Café Poca Cosa,** the creative menus change twice daily, but the commitment to fresh ingredients and authentic flavors never wavers.
110 E. Pennington Street, 520-622-6400, cafepocacosatucson.com

Elvira's, an offshoot of a now-closed longtime Nogales, Mexico, restaurant, dashes any misconceptions that mole is just a chocolate sauce.
256 E. Congress Street, 520-499-2302, elvirasrestaurant.com

Penca Restaurante offers seasonally changing dishes of central Mexico in a renovated century-old building with an air of rustic chic.
50 E. Broadway Boulevard, 520-203-7681, pencarestaurante.com

TASTE THE TOWN
WITH TUCSON FOOD TOURS

In the five-plus years that Brad Lawrence has been leading Tucson Food Tours—four-hour lunchtime strolls with stops at a half-dozen downtown eateries—the local culinary scene has taken off. So there's no dearth of material for the gregarious Tucson firefighter (and enthusiastic amateur cook) to spin his tales of city history, architecture, and culinary lore during his smooth-running rambles around town.

Along the way, there's ample time to sample an array of tasty—and ultimately filling—tidbits like slices of garlicky pizza, fried cheese curds, savory tamales, and crème-filled doughnuts. Stops range from well-known city restaurants to hidden pearls, and offer atmospheric settings, outdoor seating, secluded bars— or all three. Tour members are mostly out-of-towners, but some are local residents eager to discover the latest in downtown dining.

foodtourstucson.com

TIP
Reserve your tour at least forty-eight hours in advance.
Each tour is limited to twelve participants.

TACKLE A SONORAN
HOT DOG

The Sonoran hot dog—one of Tucson's iconic foods—is no run-of-the-mill ballpark frank. Here's the recipe: start with a hot dog, wrap it in bacon, and grill. Place into a *bolillo,* a special roll that comes with closed ends so all the toppings don't drip out.

Toppings typically include: beans, fresh onions, grilled onions, tomatoes, mayo, mustard, and hot salsa (fresh roasted chiles are optional, as are other items such as cilantro, radishes, and guacamole).

Pick it up (or grab a fork if necessary) and consume.

While you can find Sonoran hot dogs at food trucks and pop-up stands around town, Tucson has two consistently favorite purveyors:

El Güero Canelo (elguerocanelo.com) has three locations; the one on S. 12th Avenue has the most local color.

5201 S. 12th Avenue, 520-295-9005
2480 N. Oracle Road, 520-882-8977
5802 E. 22nd Street, 520-790-6000

BK Tacos (bktacos.com) has two locations:

2680 N. 1st Avenue, 520-207-2245
5118 S. 12th Avenue, 520-295-0105

STEAK YOUR CLAIM TO TRADITION
AT DAISY MAE'S

It wouldn't be cattle country without beef—or steakhouses. Some old-timers have been around since tumbleweeds drifted down Broadway Boulevard, while others are greenhorns. Daisy Mae's Steakhouse, open since 1990, falls between them in age but is a prime exemplar of this Tucson tradition.

There's nothing highbrow about the place; the most striking elements of the décor are the thousands of dollar bills with scribbled messages that have been tacked to the walls—most by patrons praising the food. Except for an extensive beer list, the menu is relatively short, focusing on beefy Angus steaks— rib eyes, T-bones, sirloins, and porterhouses expertly mesquite-grilled over an open flame—as well as tender baby back ribs and chicken with delectably crispy skin. Baked potato, ranch beans, and Texas toast are squeezed onto the platters wherever they'll fit.

2735 W. Anklam Road,
520-792-8888
daisymaessteakhouse.com

Here are other top Tucson steakhouses to try:

Charro Steak—the newest entry in the steakhouse sweepstakes—char-grills its steaks over mesquite, Sonoran-style.
188 E. Broadway Boulevard, 520-485-1922, charrosteak.com

El Corral is a venerable house of beef that rides its cowboy theme all the way and carves its signature prime rib into four sizes.
2201 E. River Road, 520-299-6092, elcorraltucson.com

Silver Saddle, another old-timer, is known for tender, flavorful rib eyes. Check out the antique mesquite bar in back.
310 E. Benson Highway, 520-622-6253, thesilversaddlesteakhouse.com

Mesquite-grilled steaks star at the **Horseshoe Grill,** which also smokes ribs, brisket, and salmon.
7713 E. Broadway Boulevard, 520-8404, thehorseshoetucson.com

GATHER IN THE COURTYARD
AT THE MERCADO

Located at the western end of the Sun Link streetcar line in a rapidly developing area on the edge of downtown Tucson, the Mercado San Agustin has established itself as a thriving Mexican-style public marketplace since opening in 2010.

You can choose among upscale New American dining at **Agustin Kitchen** (520-398-5382, agustinkitchen.com) or casual Mexican fare at **Seis Kitchen** (520-622-2002, seiskitchen.com); pick up some baked goods at **La Estrella Bakery** (520-393-3320), **Dolce Pastello Cakes** (520-207-6765), or **AKA Deli and Bakeshop** (520-369-2265); sip a coffee or Mexican hot chocolate at **Presta Coffee Roasters** (520-333-7146); cool off with *raspados* at **Sonoran Sno-Cones** (520-344-8470); and buy fresh produce at a weekly Thursday afternoon farmers' market.

100 S. Avenida del Convento
520-461-1107
mercadosanagustin.com

TIP
Table seating in the open-air inner courtyard and additional shops that sell clothing, gifts, Mexican crafts, and bicycles tempt you to linger.

SAVOR A PIE AND A PINT
AT REILLY

An Italian restaurant called Reilly? Well, yes, but that's not all that's unusual about this triple-threat establishment. Reilly Craft Pizza & Drink took its Irish-sounding name from the previous occupant, which happened to be a funeral parlor.

The main restaurant—which sports brick walls, wooden floors, and a spacious, handsome bar area of its own—serves up top-flight pizzas and pastas. The garage where the morticians kept the hearse now harbors forty taps for its craft beer offerings—many of which are served in its comfortable outdoor beer garden. And a single white arrow off the beer garden points downstairs to the speakeasy-style Tough Luck Club, where cocktails are the specialty. For an Italian restaurant named Reilly, it all makes perfect sense.

101 E. Pennington Street
520-882-5550
reillypizza.com

TIP
Be sure to try Reilly's top-selling item: fried brussels sprouts flavored with wine vinegar, hot sauce, and crumbled pecan brittle—addictive.

FEEL THE VIBE
AT SAINT CHARLES TAVERN

Tucson has its share of old favorite bars, but new waves of watering holes are making a splash by creating increasingly more inventive cocktails, uncorking regional wines, and dispensing local craft beers from the tap. Saint Charles Tavern manages to bridge the gap between the two. Though only open since 2016, it has such a casual neighborhood vibe that it feels like it's been around for years.

That neighborhood is South Tucson, a small city within the larger city—not far from downtown, replete with Mexican restaurants, but not yet gentrified. (It may, however, become Tucson's next hip hotspot). Saint Charles's welcoming service, extensive selection of cocktails and craft beers, pool tables, jukebox, outdoor area with a music stage where local bands appear, and eclectic vintage-industrial décor make for a winning combination.

1632 S. 4th Avenue
520-888-5925

Here are some more of Tucson's
"new favorite" bars to try:

At **Highwire Lounge,** you can sample the results of
"molecular mixology."
14 S. Arizona Avenue, 520-449-8673,
highwiretucson.com

Owls Club is a stylish new gathering spot with a kind
of speakeasy atmosphere,
located in a renovated mortuary.
236 S. Scott Avenue, 520-207-5678,
owlsclubwest.com

Playground has an inviting rooftop terrace
overlooking the action downtown.
278 E. Congress Street, 520-396-3691,
playgroundtucson.com

R-Bar, next to the Rialto Theatre, packs in the before-
and after-show crowds, Thursday-Saturday evenings.
350 E. Congress Street on Herbert Alley,
520-305-3599, rbartucson.com

Sky Bar is a solar-powered café by day,
and an astronomy bar by night.
536 N. 4th Avenue, 520-622-4300, skybartucson.com

Tap & Bottle pulls in the crowds
with twenty craft beers on tap.
403 N. 6th Avenue, 344-8999,
thetapandbottle.com

GO FOR THE FRIES, STAY FOR THE GREENS
AT HARVEST

You might not expect a restaurant specializing in fresh, locally sourced, and (often) organic foods to serve up some of the most addictive french fries around (thick, crunchy, and dusted with cumin and parsley). Nor might you expect that a restaurant offering top-flight burgers and sandwiches would also produce some of the best tacos and margaritas in a city replete with Mexican eateries.

But then, you might not have been to Harvest. Now in two locations—one just north of Tucson and a newer branch in the city—Harvest makes dishes from scratch and house-smokes salmon and pork. The creative burgers and tacos—the *relleno* burger and the short-rib tacos offer toothsome cross-cultural flavors—are served along with soups and organic field-greens salads, and, at dinner, seasonal entrees.

5605 E. River Road, 520-529-7180, harvestonriver.com
10355 N. La Cañada Drive, Oro Valley, 520-731-1100, harvestov.com

FIND A FOOD TRUCK
FAST

Tucson sports dozens of food trucks, serving up everything from pizza, hot dogs, burgers, and barbecue to Cajun, Vietnamese, Peruvian, and Mexican dishes. Much of it is of high quality, and some successful brick-and-mortar restaurants even operate their own trucks.

Trucks being trucks, though, they have a tendency to move around—a lot—in search of the next prime location or big event. But you don't have to go aimlessly cruising city streets to find the food truck of your dreams. The following online sites allow you to search for food trucks by type of cuisine, by current or future locations, and/or by upcoming events where they are scheduled to appear.

Tucson Food Trucks: tucsonfoodtrucks.com
Roaming Hunger: roaminghunger.com/food-trucks/az/tucson
Tucson Food Truck Roundup:
facebook.com/tucsonfoodtruckroundup

TREAT YOURSELF TO HAPPY HOUR
AT PASCO

Pasco Kitchen & Lounge, situated within a two-block commercial stretch next to the University of Arizona known as Main Gate Square, offers one of the best happy hours in Tucson. From 3 to 6 p.m. daily, Pasco serves up creative food and drink specials that fulfill the restaurant's farm to table philosophy—as illustrated by its motto, "Eat. Drink. Farm."

Owner-chef Ramiro Scavo turns out scrumptious Southwestern-inspired dishes—including some of the classiest nachos in town, available with heritage pork, free-range chicken, or organic vegetables—and some items with global accents as well. Meanwhile, Pasco's mixologists are busy creating herb-infused cocktails like the Father Kino, which fuses tequila, lime juice, and cilantro. The outdoor seating next to shady Geronimo Plaza is especially appealing here.

820 E. University Boulevard
520-882-8013
pascokitchen.com

TIP
Call 520-622-8613 for Main Gate Square information.

Main Gate Square offers a chance to munch through a variety of cuisines conveniently located for dining before or after campus events. (All are on E. University Boulevard between N. Euclid and N. Park Avenues.)

Wilko (upscale New American cooking and bar)
943 E. University Boulevard, 520-792-6684,
barwilko.com

Saigon Pho
(casual Vietnamese spot tucked down an alleyway)
943 E. University Boulevard, 520-624-0999

Kababeque (top-notch Indian takeout)
845 E. University Boulevard, 520-388-4500,
saffronaz.com

Sinbad's (Middle Eastern cuisine)
810 E. University Boulevard, 520-623-4010,
sinbadstucson.net

Espresso Art Café (coffees and hookahs)
942 E. University Avenue, 520-624-4126,
espressoartcafe.com

HAVE SOME FLAMENCO
WITH YOUR FLAN

Tucson's unofficial second language is Spanish, its history and architecture are heavily influenced by Spain, and its landscape evokes that of sun-soaked Iberia—yet there are few true Spanish restaurants here. Family-owned Casa Vicente makes up for it. Vicente himself is a Spanish native who has traveled and cooked around the world. After settling in Tucson, he and his wife, Marita, opened their restaurant specializing in tapas (small plates meant to share).

Casa Vicente also dishes up a formidable pan of paella along with full Spanish dinners, while flan and almond torte star among the house-made desserts. Wash it all down with Spanish wine or sangria to the rhythm of live music and dance on stage—including flamenco performances on some Fridays and Saturdays.

375 S. Stone Avenue
520-884-5253
casavicente.com

DIP INTO THE GUACAMOLE
AT THE FLYING V

Few things say Southwestern cuisine like guacamole, and the Flying V Bar & Grill has turned the preparation of the ever-popular avocado dip into a true tableside attraction. A "guacamoliere"—as the restaurant dubs its guacamole specialists—comes to your table with a cart of perfectly ripe avocados and additional fresh ingredients. You pick your favored condiments and level of spiciness, and the guacamoliere then fashions your made-to-order, creamily delicious dip for chips.

The Flying V is the signature restaurant at Loew's Ventana Canyon Resort in the Catalina foothills, which comes complete with mountain and city views. The rest of the menu features high-end Southwestern dishes like pasilla-rubbed calamari and shortrib tacos as well as grilled steaks, ribs, and fish. Special tequila tastings are available along with an extensive selection of margaritas.

7000 N. Resort Drive
520-615-5495
loewshotels.com/ventana-canyon

SPICE UP YOUR DAY
WITH BRUSHFIRE BBQ

Tacos, burritos, burgers, and pizza may be the top go-to choices for to-go food in Tucson, but the BrushFire BBQ Co. deserves a spot in the rotation. The slow-smoked brisket and pork are so tender and scrumptious that the BrushFire food truck gives away generous samples of each at various street fairs around town, luring many passersby to order a sandwich even if they had other lunch or dinner plans.

At BrushFire's two restaurant locations, they serve up a full menu of smoked meats and more that also includes ribs (pork or beef), chicken, turkey, salmon, pork belly, and wings. They're all given a dry rub and then gently smoked for hours before being dabbed with the sauce of your choice. A number of tasty sides are also available—as are family-sized portions.

2745 N. Campbell Avenue, 520-624-3223
7080 E. 22nd Street, 520-867-6050
brushfirebbq.com

REFRESH YOURSELF
WITH *RASPADOS*

They're one part sno-cone, one part shave ice, one part fruit-topped ice cream sundae—often with lechera (sweetened condensed milk) poured over or Mexican candies sprinkled on top—and they come in fruit-juicy flavors like mango, strawberry, pineapple, banana, cherry, lemon-lime, and blueberry.

In short, raspados may not be quite like anything you've ever tasted before—but on a hot day in Tucson, they are definitely a pleasure. The city has dozens of places to sample raspados, including

Michoacán Taqueria Raspados
(3235 N. Flowing Wells Road, 520-888-0421)

Oasis Fruit Cones
(4126 S. 12th Avenue, 520-741-7106)

Paradise Agua Frescas
(4500 N. Oracle Road in the Tucson Mall, 520-690-5763)

Raspados El Paraiso
(5917 E. 22nd Street, 520-398-5817)

Raspados La Niña
(5835 S. Park Avenue)

Sonoran Sno-Cones
(100 S. Avenida Del Convento, in the Mercado, 520-344-8470)

SEEK OUT THE "HIDDEN" DELIGHTS OF
CAFÉ A LA C'ART

Some of Tucson's top attractions harbor small restaurants and cafés that serve top-flight food but are easily overlooked by tourists and residents alike. Café a la C'Art—situated within the Tucson Museum of Art—is a prime example. Even though it's not visible from the street, the café is accessible without paying museum admission.

It's an ambitious operation, serving breakfast, lunch, and dinner and featuring a happy hour as well. Both indoor and outdoor seating are attractive options. The indoor portion is located in a historic adobe that doubles as an art gallery, while the outdoor portion occupies an inviting covered patio with a trellis in the museum's courtyard. The lunch menu, in particular, sparkles with an array of inventive sandwiches, salads, and house-made pastries—a specialty.

150 N. Main Avenue
520-628-8533
cafealacarttucson.com

Here are some other easily overlooked eateries located within various cultural attractions:

Café Botanica, within the Tucson Botanical Gardens, features delicious tacos and soups (admission to gardens required).
2150 N. Alvernon Way, 520-326-9686, tucsonbotanical.org/cafe

La Cocina Restaurant, offering eclectic Latin-flavored dishes, occupies a secluded courtyard within the Old Town Artisans shopping complex.
201 N. Court Avenue, 520-622-0351, lacocinatucson.com

Simplicit is a comfortable, greenery-filled bistro serving Mediterranean cuisine at the Temple of Music and Art.
330 S. Scott Avenue, 520-884-0238, simplicitrestaurant.com

The Garden Bistro at Tohono Chul serves "breakfast with butterflies," lunch, and Sunday brunch.
7366 N. Paseo del Norte, 520-742-6455, tohonochulpark.org

TRAIN YOUR APPETITE FOR A FEAST
AT MAYNARDS

Located within Tucson's 1907-era Historic Train Depot, Maynards Market & Kitchen offers a close-up view of the many trains that rumble through the city. Chances are, though, you'll be paying such rapt attention to your food—some of the city's finest and freshest cuisine—that the trains will have passed before you notice.

The Kitchen is open nightly for dinner (preceded by a two-hour Happy Hour) and Sunday brunch, serving "Old World" specialties—cassoulet, pan-roasted duck, bouillabaisse—with locally sourced ingredients. At Sunday brunch, you can sit inside or out on the patio by the tracks, savoring the baked eggs, one of the city's best brunch dishes.

The self-service Market, open for three casual meals a day with patio seating, serves up inventive sandwiches—the Cubano and the grilled veggie stand out—as well as flavorful soups and salads.

400 N. Toole Avenue
520-545-0577
maynardstucson.com

TIP

After your meal, you may want to explore the renovated Historic Train Depot, view the 1900-era engine of Locomotive 1673 (which appeared in the film *Oklahoma!*), and tour the little Southern Arizona Transportation Museum (414 N. Toole Avenue), crammed with railway memorabilia.

MUSIC AND ENTERTAINMENT

PUNCH YOUR TICKET
TO BROADWAY
IN TUCSON

A staple of top-quality entertainment since 2004, Broadway in Tucson has moved from the Tucson Music Hall in the downtown Convention Center to 2,500-seat Centennial Hall on the University of Arizona campus. Each season, which extends from September to the following April, brings a half dozen or so nationally touring productions of hit Broadway shows past and present, sometimes featuring stars direct from the originals.

Broadway in Tucson productions have included *The Lion King, Mamma Mia, Cabaret, Phantom of the Opera, West Side Story, Fiddler on the Roof, The Sound of Music, Avenue Q, Motown: The Musical, and Kinky Boots*—selling out many engagements and drawing audiences totaling more than 425,000 people. Centennial Hall, which dates from 1937, has excellent sight lines to the stage and completed major acoustics upgrades in 2007.

1020 E. University Boulevard
800-745-3000 (tickets),
broadwayintucson.com

BE MYSTIFIED
AT CARNIVAL OF ILLUSION

It's an evening of "Old World Magic" with healthy doses of mystery, danger, and "ooh la la" tossed in. And Carnival of Illusion—a two-person show performed by the engaging couple Roland Sarlot and Susan Eyed—delivers plenty of laughs and vaudeville-style showmanship to boot.

Playing off a Victorian-era world travel theme, Sarlot and Eyed smoothly deliver a slew of "how did they do that?" magical moments—pulling off sleight-of-hand, card, and memory tricks; swallowing razor blades; defying gravity; cutting a woman in half; and making U.S. currency miraculously appear inside freshly cut fruit. There's plenty of audience participation along the way as well. Everyone leaves smiling—and suitably mystified.

Carnival of Illusion appears on select Saturdays during the year on an intimate stage in the ornate Scottish Rite Grand Parlour in downtown Tucson.

160 S. Scott Street
520-615-5299
carnivalofillusion.com

SET YOUR CALENDAR
FOR 2ND SATURDAYS

The concept is simple: line up some bands to provide live music on multiple stages downtown; invite food trucks to serve concessions; coordinate with nearby restaurants, attractions, and businesses; and give it a name everyone will remember. That name—"2nd Saturdays"—even marks your calendar for you, since these free outdoor street festivals take place the second Saturday of every month.

The music varies—you may find a punk rock band on one stage, a Pink Floyd cover band or an all-female surf rock band on another—and the evening hours vary somewhat by season (earlier in winter, later in summer). But the formula remains the same: offer quality, family-friendly music and food, and they will come—every 2nd Saturday.

E. Congress Street and S. Scott Avenue, downtown
520-268-9030
2ndsaturdays.com

TUNE IN TO THE
TUCSON SYMPHONY

Back in 1929, when the Tucson Symphony Orchestra (TSO) tuned up its first violins, it was a group composed of mostly amateur musicians playing in a school auditorium. Today, as a highly accomplished professional orchestra whose main venue is the nearly 3,000-seat Music Hall at the Tucson Convention Center, it performs a number of "Classic" and "MasterWorks" concerts each season (September through April) along with a variety of ensemble performances and chamber orchestra, pops, and children's concerts. It's also added a Youth Orchestra and Symphony Chorus.

The TSO also periodically plays in smaller area venues: a high school, a church, its own Symphony Center, and even at top local restaurants for its "Moveable Musical Feasts." Each holiday season, the Symphony Chorus performs Handel's *Messiah* accompanied by the symphony's Chamber Orchestra.

Tucson Music Hall: 260 S. Church Avenue
Box Office: 2175 N. 6th Avenue, 520-882-8585
tucsonsymphony.org

TIP
The Symphony offers a number of handy "Create Your Own Journey" options for buying partial season tickets; for example, you could choose a package of "My Generation" concerts—such as Country Legends and The Music of the Who—or "Giants," such as Beethoven, Brahms, and Tchaikovsky.

FIND A WEALTH OF FLICKS
AT THE LOFT CINEMA

Tucson has plenty of cookie-cutter multiplexes airing many of the same blockbuster movies, but if you're yearning for something different, head to the Loft Cinema. Since 1972, the Loft has been treating Tucsonans to the best—and often the most offbeat—movies ever made. Whether it's current or classic cinema, foreign or domestic, Hollywood or indie, musicals or documentaries, commercial or art films, the Loft has it all—and shows them on the largest screen in southern Arizona. Expert commentary accompanies some screenings.

Among their ongoing series are Cult Classics *(Harold and Maude, Bladerunner)* and Mondo Mondays (horror films). On some Friday nights, they invite would-be auteurs to submit their own short films for showings, but if you're among them, be forewarned—if the audience doesn't like it, you'll get gonged.

3233 E. Speedway Boulevard
520-795-0844
loftcinema.org

TIP

Tucson hosts the eleven day Arizona International Film Festival in late April each year. Geared toward independent films, it's the oldest and largest film fest in the state. And each March, Tucson Cine Mexico adds to its standing as the longest-running festival of contemporary Mexican cinema in the country.

Other places to find distinctive film-going experiences include:

The **RoadHouse Cinema,** where you can recline your seat, put your feet up, and order food and drink to be brought to you during the show.
4811 E. Grant Road, 520-468-7980,
roadhousecinemas.com

Cinema La Placita, which shows $3 outdoor movies downtown every Thursday at 7:30 p.m. from May to August, and even throws in the popcorn.
cinemalaplacita.com

GO FOR PROVOKE
AT THE ROGUE

Performing in an intimate venue converted from a former gym, the Rogue Theatre presents a lively and eclectic assortment of five plays each season from September to May. For more than a decade, the talented ensembles have served up award-winning, innovative productions ranging from classical to modern-day dramatists. (One Shakespeare play is on the docket every year.)

Why "Rogue"? The Latin origin of "rogue"—*rogare*—means "to ask," and the company regards its mission as presenting plays that offer challenging and provocative points of view. But while it takes its mission seriously, it also retains a puckish sense of humor. One recent production, *Penelope,* about conniving suitors pursuing Odysseus's wife during the Trojan War hero's long absence, sets the action in a swimming pool—with the actors clad in Speedos.

300 E. University Boulevard
520-344-8715; box office: 520-551-2053
theroguetheatre.org

TIP
Tickets are general admission except those reserved for season ticket holders. But in this cozy, comfortable theater, all seats offer excellent viewing.

RETURN TO YESTERYEAR
AT "HOLLYWOOD IN THE DESERT"

John Wayne wore his chaps and holsters here. Clint Eastwood, Elizabeth Taylor, and the casts of TV's *Bonanza* and *Little House on the Prairie* donned their spurs and crinolines for roles in classic Westerns. For more than seventy-five years, Old Tucson Studios has served as the saguaro-studded stage for over 400 Hollywood films and other productions, and remains a working set.

Now, though, Old Tucson is also an Old West theme park, complete with dramatized gunfights, stunt shows, and more. Ride a train, horse, or an antique carousel. Drive a horseless carriage, pan for gold, or test your aim at the shooting gallery. Listen up as historians spin Western lore. Grab a sarsaparilla or some suds at the saloon. Chow down on barbecue. And stock up on souvenirs at the local mercantile. Just steer clear of the bad guys at High Noon.

201 S. Kinney Road
520-883-0100
oldtucson.com

CATCH A CLASSIC
AT THE ATC

Splitting its time between Tucson and Phoenix, the Arizona Theatre Company (ATC) has produced well over 200 plays in its more than half century history. Performing on the main stage in Tucson's historic Temple of Music and Art, the ATC's professional cast and staff have staged works ranging from classic Shakespeare and Molière to contemporary playwrights like Shepard and Fugard. Musicals and lighter fare are also on the docket. Almost all the costumes, sets, and props are produced in-house.

With its front courtyard, fountain, and Mexican tile, the Spanish Colonial Revival-style Temple of Music and Art makes an attractive venue. Besides the main 623-seat Alice Holsclaw Theatre, the Temple also houses the 80-seat Cabaret Theatre, an art gallery, and the attractive Simplicit restaurant. The annual theater season runs from September to April.

330 S. Scott Avenue
520-622-2823
arizonatheatre.org

MAKE YOUR WAY
TO THE MONTEREY COURT CAFÉ

It's easy to drive past the Monterey Court Café and never realize that one of Tucson's most enjoyable music venues lies hidden within. A neon sign still reads "Monterey Court," a 1938-built motel that sat at the eastern end of the Miracle Mile, once one of the city's prime lodging strips. In 2011, the motel closed and was transformed into an artisan enclave complete with music stage, galleries, shops, and a café serving upscale food and drink.

The dining patio offers good views of the courtyard stage, where live music is presented every evening Tuesday through Sunday. Open-air or covered seating can accommodate up to 300 people. Musical genres vary nightly—you may encounter jazz, blues, Western swing, African soul, rockabilly, or anything else. There's also a music brunch every Sunday.

505 W. Miracle Mile
520-207-2429
montereycourtaz.com

TIP
It's always a good idea to call for reservations here.

TAKE IN TOP ACTS
WITH UA PRESENTS

The University of Arizona offers a treasure trove of music and other entertainment on campus, including performances by world-renowned artists as well as by talented students and faculty members.

The headlining shows are brought in under the umbrella of UA Presents, which attracts top-name entertainers—singers, dancers, musicians, and more—to perform in varying venues, mostly on campus. Recent shows have run the gamut of star power from the Warsaw Philharmonic Orchestra and violinist Itzhak Perlman to singer Chaka Khan, "Godmother of Soul" Bettye LaVette to the Peking Acrobats. Campus venues include the 2,500-seat Centennial Hall, 600-seat Crowder Hall, and the 295-seat Stevie Eller Dance Theatre. Some shows are staged at the 1,164-seat Fox Tucson Theatre downtown.

520-621-3341
uapresents.org

Lesser-known campus productions range from drama to music and dance:

At the **Arizona Repertory Theatre,** UA theater majors perform on stage and off in six main productions each season—one always a Shakespeare play.
Marroney Theatre and the Tornabene Theatre, 520-621-1162, theatre.arizona.edu/venues

The **Fred Fox School of Music** presents concerts and recitals by UA faculty and students, as well as guest artists.
Fine Arts Complex and other campus locations.
520-621-1655, music.arizona.edu

The **UA Dance Ensemble** features professionally trained student dancers performing ballet, modern, and jazz dance.
Stevie Eller Dance Theatre,
1713 E. University Boulevard, 520-621-1162, tickets.arizona.edu

HEIGH-HO,
COME TO THE FAIR

Tucson's largest family-oriented event, the Pima County Fair, has been packing in the crowds since 1911. An annual week-long blowout, it lights up the Pima County Fairgrounds in late April.

Carnival rides and games, concerts large and small— including the likes of Tanya Tucker and the Village People at recent fairs—percussive dance performances, petting zoos, kiddie areas, tractor pulls, rodeos, antique car shows, horse shows, pony rides, sea lion encounters, wildlife exhibits, animal barns, livestock auctions, demolition derbies, and beer fests are all typically on tap.

And what would a county fair be without a sideshow or a hypnotist? Well, probably a good excuse to do all those other things plus chow down on guilty-pleasure food that you might never eat except at the Pima County Fair.

11300 S. Houghton Road
520-762-3247
pimacountyfair.com

TIP
The fair is located one mile south of I-10 and the Houghton Road exit.

GUSSY UP
FOR THE OPERA

Prepare to be swept away by the majesty of vibrant baritones, soaring sopranos, and vivid costuming and sets. In its four and a half decades, the Arizona Opera Company has produced more than 170 fully staged operas and concerts and now presents five grand operas each fall-to-spring season at the Tucson Music Hall in the Convention Center.

Recent productions include *Madama Butterfly, Rigoletto, Carmen, Don Giovanni,* and *Tosca,* as well as operettas and operas by Arizona composers. Arizona Opera has also staged Wagner's demanding four-opera *Ring Cycle* twice—a feat accomplished by just a handful of other American opera companies. Musicians drawn from three Arizona symphony orchestras as well as a chorus of talented local vocalists add depth to the productions.

260 S. Church Avenue (Tucson Music Hall)
Box office: 520-293-4336
azopera.org

TIP
Never fear if you aren't fluent in the many languages of opera. English translations are displayed on a screen above the stage as the performers vocalize, and the printed programs contain synopses of the often complex and scandalous plots.

MOSEY ON OVER
TO THE MAVERICK

After the rodeo—or just when you have a hankerin' for two-stepping out on the town—Tucson's Maverick Live Country Club has been the place to go for more than fifty-five years. The east side night club features a different activity or special each of the five nights they're open during the week. You could opt for "2-4-1" drinks on Tuesdays, line dancing on Wednesdays, Ladies (free) Nights on Thursdays, bargain beers on Fridays, or dancing to Flipside (a local cover band) on Saturdays.

You can also take dance lessons here—so you and your partner can tune up your two-step or master the art of line dancing. Along with ample supplies of beer and margaritas, the Maverick offers a dinner menu of appetizers, sandwiches, and entrées.

6622 E. Tanque Verde Road
520-298-0430
tucsonmaverick.com

CRUISE TO A CONCERT
ON CONGRESS

Two legendary Congress Street grand-dame theaters with similar histories—the Fox and the Rialto—have been key to the revival of downtown Tucson as a thriving entertainment hub.

The art deco **Fox Tucson Theatre**—once dubbed downtown's "Crown Jewel"—dates from 1930, when it was a movie and vaudeville venue. After the mid-1970s, it was closed for thirty years before being extensively restored in 2006. The 1,164-seat theater now presents nationally known musical acts, theatrical productions, and film screenings.

17 W. Congress Street, 520-547-3040, foxtucson.com

The 1,200-seat **Rialto Theatre** debuted in the 1920s hosting silent movies and vaudeville acts. After extensive renovations in the 1990s and 2000s, it now attracts about 200 musical acts annually— indie and rock bands, jazz musicians, country singers, and more— along with other entertainers.

318 E. Congress Street, 520-740-1000, rialtotheatre.com

COZY UP TO THE BANDS
AT 191 TOOLE

You should be able to find 191 Toole—its address is its name. (Technically, the address is 191 E. Toole.) And once you get there, you'll find free parking and a lot to like. The sound system and acoustics are first-rate, the staff is friendly, and most concerts are open to all ages. Tickets and beer are reasonably priced, the restrooms clean. The maximum number of concert-goers is 500. And they attract some top regional and local bands.

There is one drawback, at least for some older music fans: it's almost entirely standing room only. It can also get hot in summer when it fills up. But if you want to hear Micky and the Motorcars, Chicano Batman, or CJ Ramone as they were meant to be heard, 191 Toole is the place.

191 E. Toole Avenue
520-445-6425
191toole.com

You might also like these other small-to-medium–sized music venues:

Club Congress, located in the historic Hotel Congress, features live music some nights and DJs spinning dance tunes on others. Watch for the free outdoor
Spring Concert Series.
311 E. Congress Street, 520-622-8848,
hotelcongress.com/club

Since 2014, **The Flycatcher** has been luring local, regional, and national touring acts to its hip bar and lounge. In good weather, head for the outdoor patio near the stage.
340 E. 6th Street, 520-207-9251
(tickets: 877-435-9849),
flycatchertucson.com

HAVE A GUFFAW
AT THE GASLIGHT

Don't go to the Gaslight Theatre expecting serious drama—but you can expect some seriously funny melodrama, set to the often boisterous backdrop of a tinny piano, corny jokes, and audience laughter. Staging five original shows per year—often musical spoofs of popular movies (*Space Wars, Back to the Past*)—Gaslight has developed a devoted clientele while honing its shtick since 1977. Feel free to cheer the good guys and boo the villains—audience participation is encouraged.

Table seating permits you to munch and sip suds or soda along with the action on stage. While the performers are more polished than the food—pizza, nachos, and such—it's fine for a casual, family-friendly meal (and the popcorn is free). Each production, including an annual Christmas show, runs six nights a week for two to three months.

7010 E. Broadway Boulevard
520-886-9428
thegaslighttheatre.com

TIP
Mondays at Gaslight are concert nights—
often tributes to country, rock, or pop music artists.

DIVE INTO DANCE
AT THE BALLET

Ballet Tucson brings high-quality dance to the desert, producing a mix of classical and contemporary ballets each season (November to May). Founded in 1986, Ballet Tucson developed into a fully professional dance troupe by 2004, and now its roster has two dozen artists who have danced professionally with companies throughout the United States.

As part of its cultural mission and community outreach programs, the ballet company also nurtures a children's ensemble that performs alongside the pros in productions such as *Cinderella, Sleeping Beauty,* and its annual holiday presentation of the *Nutcracker.* Performances take place in major venues around the city, including the Temple of Music and Art, the Tucson Music Hall, and the Stevie Eller Dance Theatre.

520-903-1445
ballettucson.org

SWAY TO THE MUSIC
AT THE DESERT SONG FESTIVAL

In much of the United States, summertime is music festival season. Not so in Tucson, where musicians gather in cooler months to celebrate life with instrument and song. The Tucson Desert Song Festival has blossomed quickly from its inaugural year of 2013 into a city-wide musical extravaganza that extends for three weeks from January into February and has attracted talent of international stature in multiple genres.

Performers have included Broadway's Bernadette Peters, Metropolitan Opera mezzo-soprano Jennifer Johnson Cano, guitarists Rene Izquierdo and Adam del Monte, and pianists Michael Barrett and Steven Blier. Vocalists from pop to classical, chamber orchestras, ballet troupes, medieval ensembles, and tributes to artists such as Leonard Bernstein appear in city venues large and small, from the spacious Tucson Music Hall and Fox Tucson Theatre to the more intimate Leo Rich Theater and Temple of Music and Art.

tucsondesertsongfestival.org

You can also check out these other
great seasonal music festivals:

Tucson Jazz Festival: Jazz junkies gather at venues
around the city each January for ten days of concerts
that span most every genre.
tucsonjazzfestival.org

Gem and Jam Fest: Coinciding with Tucson's huge
Gem and Mineral Showcase each February, this four-
day fest features everything from acid rock to reggae,
bluegrass fusion to funk, afrobeat to disco.
Pima County Fairground, gemandjamfestival.com

Tucson Folk Festival: One of the largest free folk
music festivals in the country attracts musicians from
throughout the Southwest for two days of music and
dance in early May, at several different venues.
tucsonfolkfest.org

HIT THE TRAIL
TO TRAIL DUST TOWN

If it weren't surrounded by the rest of Tucson, Trail Dust Town might eventually evolve into Trail Dust Metropolis. Opening in 1961 with a steakhouse and some shops bearing an Old West theme, Trail Dust Town has mushroomed over the decades into a family-friendly (and family-owned) entertainment complex that includes live Western stunt shows, amusement park rides (including a Ferris wheel and an antique carousel), a railroad, a haunted house, a U.S. military museum, a gold-panning area, a shooting gallery, a day spa, a saloon, a weekly farmers' market, and an old-time photography studio—as well as the "pioneer-era" shops and steakhouse that started it all.

Trail Dust Town doesn't come fully alive until the evenings; hours vary by the activity and season, so check their website for each.

6541 E. Tanque Verde Road
520-296-4551
traildusttown.com

TIP
You can pay by the individual activity or purchase unlimited access to most attractions for an entire evening.

HEAR THE VOICES OF THE BORDER
AT BORDERLANDS

Borderlands Theater didn't choose its name lightly. Founded in 1986, this Tucson-based professional company has focused most of its productions on the people who live in the U.S.-Mexico border region, with special emphasis on Latino and Native cultures.

With the goal of creating greater understanding within the borderlands and giving voice to often overlooked segments of the population, it has developed and produced dozens of plays by new and established playwrights on topics as weighty as immigration and as intimate as daily life. But it also stages an annual light-hearted holiday season show called A Tucson Pastorela, lampooning the year's most lampoon-able events.

Borderlands productions appear in venues around the city, including the Cabaret Theatre in the Temple of Music and Art downtown, and some unexpected settings like Saguaro National Park—complete with cactus backdrop.

Tickets: 520-882-7406
borderlandstheater.org

GAMBLE AND GAMBOL
AT TUCSON'S CASINOS

Local Native American tribes own and operate two prominent casinos on tribal lands just outside Tucson, which serve up the requisite games of chance and more.

The **Casino Del Sol Resort,** run by the Pascua Yaqui Tribe, has branched out beyond its 1,300 slot machines and 22 table games, staging concerts and other productions at the 5,000-seat AVA Amphitheater as well as live music at the smaller Paradiso Bar & Lounge.

5655 W. Valencia Road, 855-765-7829, casinodelsolresort.com

Over at the **Desert Diamond Casinos & Entertainment,** owned and operated by the Tohono O'odham Nation, they're promising Arizona's "biggest uncapped jackpots," with poker, blackjack, bingo, and Keno all featuring high-stakes games. After testing your luck, celebrate or commiserate at the Monsoon Nightclub, which hosts a variety of national musical acts.

7350 S. Nogales Highway (I-19), one mile south of Valencia Road, 866-332-9467, ddcaz.com

SPORTS AND RECREATION

EXPLORE
A DESERT OASIS

For many Tucsonans, hiking and Sabino Canyon are virtually synonymous. With its palm trees, creeks, hillside cacti, picnic areas, and glimpses of local wildlife, the Sabino Canyon Recreation Area is a place to escape urban life just a few minutes' drive from the city. It lies in the Coronado National Forest in the foothills of the Santa Catalina Mountains, and it is crisscrossed with trails ranging from easy nature walks to steep, rugged treks.

Transportation to upper Sabino Canyon—where many of the trails lie—is restricted to hikers, cyclists, and tram shuttle riders. The narrated 45-minute, 3.8-mile-long tram service makes nine stops and operates daily every half hour. Passengers can stay on the tram or get off at any stop and hike the trails, hike back to the Visitor's Center, or catch the tram back from any stop.

5700 N. Sabino Canyon Road
520-749-8700 (Tram: 520-749-2861)
sabinocanyon.com

TIP
Some of the trails are risky in high water and the road to Upper Sabino Canyon may flood at points as well. Waterproof shoes come in handy in winter to spring; carry plenty of drinking water every season.

ELEVATE YOUR DAY
ON MT. LEMMON

Tucsonans head here in summer to escape the heat, and in winter to ski in the snow. In the spring and fall, they seek out its hiking trails and take in the panoramic views of Tucson and beyond. Birders add to their life lists here, while rock hounds admire its striking geological formations.

Mt. Lemmon—the highest peak in the Santa Catalina range at 9,147 feet—looms some 7,000 feet above Tucson's northern foothills and offers recreational opportunities at every elevation and season. Allow plenty of time to drive to the top up the long, twisting road. Or, if you're biking it—well, good luck.

Once there, the small community of Summerhaven offers a few restaurants, shops, and services. Dress in layers even in summer—a ninety degree day in Tucson might be sixty degrees at the summit.

Catalina Highway (Mt. Lemmon Scenic Byway)
520-576-9147
hikelemmon.com

TIP
The ski area is the southernmost in the country; on a sunny winter day, you could conceivably hit Tucson's tennis courts in the morning and Mt. Lemmon's ski slopes later that day.

VISIT THE DARK SIDE FOR
STARRY, STARRY NIGHTS

The International Dark Sky Association—dedicated to fighting the light pollution that obscures the starry nights of yore—was founded in Tucson. And while the city's growth means it's not quite the low-light city of years past, star-gazing opportunities still abound under the region's night skies.

You might opt for a periodic ranger- or naturalist-led "Star Party" or "Night Walk" in Saguaro National Park East, a "Silhouettes at Sundown" walk in Saguaro National Park West, or a "Cool Summer Nights" visit to the Arizona-Sonora Desert Museum for views of sunsets, stars, and nocturnal creatures May to September.

Or you could head up to the Mt. Lemmon Sky Center for star gazing high above the city, or out to the Kitt Peak National Observatory in the high desert west of Tucson, where state-of-the-art telescopes await.

Saguaro National Park: 520-733-5153 (East), 520-733-5158 (West)

Arizona-Sonora Desert Museum: 2021 N. Kinney Road, 520-883-2702, desertmuseum.org

Mt. Lemmon Sky Center: 520-626-8122, skycenter.arizona.edu

Kitt Peak National Observatory: (reservations required) 520-318-8726, (recorded info: 520-318-8200), noao.edu

HEAD UNDERGROUND
AT KARTCHNER CAVERNS

Had it not been for two young explorers who happened upon a tiny passageway leading underground back in 1974, we might never have known about their remarkable find: the vast, pristine "live" cave system now known as Kartchner Caverns. Remarkably, the men kept their discovery secret for fourteen more years, and it wasn't until 1999 that the site opened to the public as a state park.

The caverns are known for their strange and colorful limestone formations, including long, icicle-thin stalactites and drapes that resemble bacon and noodles. Two separate half-mile-long guided tours lead you through. One includes the discoverers' original trail, while another focuses on some of the most unusual formations. Special tours—exploring with only light from headlamps—are offered on Saturdays. The park also features campgrounds, hiking trails, and picnicking.

Take I-10 east forty-one miles to AZ-90 (exit 302) near Benson; go south on AZ-90 nine miles and follow the signs into the state park.

877-586-2283 (reservations)
azstateparks.com/kartchner

TIP
People with mobility, respiratory, or claustrophobia problems, as well as young children, may have difficulty in some of the caves' dimly lit, narrow passages. Some tours have minimum age restrictions.

DISCOVER LIFE
AT THE DESERT MUSEUM

Tucson is all about life in the desert, so it's appropriate that the Arizona- Sonora Desert Museum is the city's top visitor attraction. Forget any preconceptions about the desert being a stark place with little plant and animal life. And put aside any notions that this is a typical museum—the Desert Museum is primarily an outdoor experience, covering 21 acres and harboring some 1,200 types of plants and 300 animal species.

Besides enjoying exceptional views of mountains and valleys, you can follow trails to watch for wildcats, coyotes, and bighorn sheep; enter an aviary where native hummingbirds fly freely around you; stroll through a landscaped cactus garden; and head underground to encounter creatures that emerge only in the dark of night. You'll discover that the desert is a thriving complex ecosystem—and anything but deserted.

2021 N. Kinney Road
520-883-2702
desertmuseum.org

TIP
To best adapt to desert life yourself, wear a hat, sunscreen, and good walking shoes, and take advantage of the shaded ramadas and drinking fountains scattered throughout the facility.

GO GLOBAL
AT THE INTERNATIONAL WILDLIFE MUSEUM

Though not far down the road from the better-known Arizona-Sonora Desert Museum, the International Wildlife Museum is (you might say) a completely different animal. The former has live desert animals, while at the latter, all the wildlife on display are permanent taxidermied residents from around the globe.

That said, the International Wildlife Museum's 400-plus collection of preserved mammals, birds, and insects (all donated after their deaths) reside in well-designed exhibits and have the advantage of always being visible when you visit—plus you can view them up close without fear of a lion snacking on your arm.

Kids, especially, may be surprised to see just how big some animals (including a few prehistoric creatures) are at close range. The museum prides itself on supporting wildlife conservation efforts and educational outreach programs for children.

4800 W. Gates Pass Road
520-629-0100
thewildlifemuseum.org

TIP
The museum shows movies like *Creepy Creatures* and *Animal Mysteries* daily in its Wildlife Theater.

HIKE THE
CATALINA CANYONS

Situated on one-time ranchland on the western edges of the Santa Catalina Mountains, Catalina State Park encompasses more than 5,000 acres leading up into craggy foothills and canyons. The park is thick with cacti—including thousands of majestic saguaros—and tall, slender ocotillos. In winter and spring, water courses through the canyons, feeding streams, pools, and waterfalls.

Short nature trails near the main trailhead provide a good introduction, but for serious hikers the rugged, often steep 5.5-mile round-trip hike to Romero Pools via the Romero Canyon Trail ranks as one of the region's most beautiful treks—with sweeping views punctuated by saguaros, boulders, strikingly green desert vegetation (in season), and the refreshing sounds of rushing water. You might even spot bighorn sheep.

11570 N. Oracle Road
520-628-5798
azstateparks.com/catalina

TIP
The park also offers camping, picnicking, birding, and horseback riding.

DRIFT OVER THE DESERT
IN A BALLOON

Drifting over the Tucson Mountains and Saguaro National Park West in a hot air balloon at sunrise is an unforgettable experience, and long-time balloon pilot Mike Fleury promises a safe, smooth, highly scenic ride for his four-to-five-passenger flights. Fleur de Tucson balloons ascend to heights ranging from 500 to 2,500 feet, permitting both close-up views of desert wildlife—perhaps javelinas, bobcats, foxes, and red-tailed hawks—as well as sweeping panoramas.

The sixty- to seventy-five minute rides travel from ten to eighteen miles, varying with the wind currents. Safety comes first: balloons don't take off in strong winds, and Fleur de Tucson boasts an accident-free record. Fleury's wife, Becky, drives the "chase truck," which meets the balloon where it lands and carries champagne and breakfast fare to celebrating passengers. Due to summer heat, ballooning season runs from October to mid-April.

520-403-8547
fleurdetucson.net

TIP
Families are welcome (minimum age 3); weight limit per passenger is 275 pounds.

TACKLE TUMAMOC HILL
FOR A SCENIC WORKOUT

Every week year-round, thousands of Tucsonans of all ages, body types, and fashion tastes set out to climb to the top of 3,100-foot-high Tumamoc Hill on the city's west side. A wide roadway leads one-and-a-half miles to the summit, 800 feet above the base, via a series of increasingly steep switchbacks.

The paved surface is well suited to the intrepid cardio hounds who run the route or push baby strollers. But most climbers take time to catch their breaths and enjoy the hillside desert vegetation—cacti, ocotillos, palo verde trees—and watch for wildlife such as deer, rabbits, and reptiles. Those who reach the top are rewarded with sweeping views of the city and surrounding mountains—and can take comfort in the reassuring knowledge that the return is all downhill.

W. Anklam Road and Tumamoc Hill Road

TIP
While you can tackle Tumamoc any time on Saturdays and Sundays, during the rest of the week the route is off limits from 7:30 a.m. to 5:30 p.m. (it's a University of Arizona ecological research center). Sunrise and sunset are prime climb times.

BROWSE THE BEAUTY
OF THE BOTANICAL GARDENS

The Tucson Botanical Gardens displays an alluring array of desert plant life in the heart of the city. The five-and-a-half-acre gardens are divided into seventeen specialty sections that illuminate a stunning variety of vegetation found in southern Arizona and in desert climes around the world.

They include crops and medicinal plants used by Native Americans, traditional Mexican-American neighborhood gardens, a children's discovery garden, a backyard bird garden, a miniature train garden, a Zen garden, a prehistoric garden, and (October through May) a delightful tropical butterfly and orchid pavilion.

But the crown jewel is the cactus and succulents garden, showcasing dozens of species of cacti and related plants—both regional and from as far away as North Africa. An art gallery and top-notch gift shop and café add to the attractions.

2150 N. Alvernon Way
520-326-9686
tucsonbotanical.org

TIP
Watch for special exhibitions from October through May, as well as periodic guided tours.

WANDER THE DESERT GARDENS
OF TOHONO CHUL

Along Tucson's northern fringes lie forty-five acres of botanical gardens and desert landscapes, honeycombed with walking paths and nature trails. At Tohono Chul Park, stroll through a desert palm oasis and a hummingbird garden, visit a "geology wall" built from rock specimens in the nearby mountains, and take your kids to a children's garden. Or tour an "ethnobotanical" garden displaying plants the local Tohono O'odham tribe employed to make medicines and baskets, and discover how to create a *sin agua* (without water) garden as well as a Desert Living Courtyard at home.

Much of the emphasis is on learning how to nurture your own garden in the desert. Suitably inspired, you can purchase a wide range of cacti and other native plants from the greenhouse there, or browse the top-flight gift shop.

7366 N. Paseo del Norte
520-742-6455
tohonochulpark.org

TIP
Each year in mid-December, Tohono Chul stages its Holiday Nights spectacular, filling the gardens with more than a million twinkling lights, along with strolling musicians and food.

FIND HANDS-ON FUN
AT THE CHILDREN'S MUSEUM

The best children's museums combine learning with fun, and the Children's Museum Tucson—whose focus is on creative play with a purpose—does exactly that. Since moving into the 1900-era former Carnegie Library building downtown in 1991, the action-packed museum has provided children of all ages (and their parents!) with rooms full of imaginative, hands-on displays and activities.

Art and architecture projects, science experiments, garden adventures, model train engineering, and much more help kids and families discover and explore a variety of fascinating new worlds. In Wee World, preschoolers have their own toy kitchen, climbing structures, slides, and soft building blocks. The museum also sponsors a busy calendar of special events and classes, ranging from yoga to math and even to "grossology"—lessons on the workings of the human digestive system.

200 S. 6th Avenue
520-792-9985
childrensmuseumtucson.org

ZIP OVER
TO THE REID PARK ZOO

Back in 1969, when it first opened its doors, the Reid Park Zoo was more like a glorified backyard menagerie than a real zoo. As the zookeepers describe it, they had only "birds, prairie dogs, farm animals, a few squirrel monkeys." But over the years the now fully accredited zoo has spread across twenty-four acres that harbor hundreds of animals and attract some 600,000 annual visitors.

Elephants, grizzlies, lions, tigers, rhinos, zebras, giraffes, lemurs, gibbons, macaques, ostriches, flamingos, tortoises, bearded dragons, skinks, macaws, and meerkats all make their homes here. There are also two aviaries: one with birds of the world and another with South American species. Giraffe Encounters, camel rides, the Zoo Train, and carousel rides—with thirty different species like anteaters and polar bears going round and round—are additional features.

3400 E. Zoo Court
520-791-3204
reidparkzoo.org

TIP
If your kids really love the carousel, it might pay to buy a Zoo-It-All daily pass, which includes unlimited carousel rides (all thirty species?) plus one camel ride and one train ride.

SOJOURN WITH
THE DESERT SENTINELS

Saguaros, the stately cacti that have served as the backdrop for countless western movies, are found only in the Sonoran Desert, where Tucson resides. With their characteristic "arms," heights up to fifty feet, and lifespans up to 200 years, saguaros have been dubbed the Sentinels of the Desert—standing watch, in effect, over all other life forms in this arid land.

To view them in their greatest natural splendor here, head to Saguaro National Park. Spread over a total of more than 90,000 acres, Saguaro is actually two parks in one—West and East, separated by about thirty miles of urbanity and nestled in the foothills of two mountain ranges. Saguaro East is larger, but both offer multiple ways of exploring their saguaro forests: scenic roadways, hiking trails, nature walks, horseback rides, and picnic spots.

Saguaro East: 3693 S. Old Spanish Trail, 520-733-5153
Saguaro West: 2700 N. Kinney Road, 520-733-5158
nps.gov/sagu

TIP
Best months to visit—for cooler weather and more scheduled activities—are October to April.

SPEND A WEEKEND
WITH WILDCAT FOOTBALL

On six or seven weekends from September through November, home football games at 56,000-seat Arizona Stadium blossom into social occasions as much as sporting events. On Bear Down Fridays, the day before each Saturday game, a block party complete with marching band and cheerleaders breaks out in Main Gate Square at the western end of campus.

Then on game days come the immensely popular tailgate parties on the UA Mall—when hundreds of beer and barbecue celebrants set up their tents. Finally, the Wildcat Walk features the players strolling to the nearby stadium to the cheers and high-fives of fans. Once inside the stadium, a 112-foot-tall, 47-foot wide video board—one of the largest and loudest in college football—sets the tone for the on-field action.

arizonawildcats.com

TIP
Why is "Bear Down" the UA motto when the mascot is the Wildcat? The tradition stems from the dying words of a popular UA athlete back in 1926, who urged his teammates to "bear down"—and his exhortation stuck.

CATCH THE CATS
PLAYING HOOPS

The toughest tickets to land in Tucson between October and March are for seats at University of Arizona men's basketball games. After decades of fielding highly ranked teams, the Wildcats regularly fill 14,545-seat McKale Center, especially when playing Pacific 12 Conference rivals. A raucous group of students dubbed the ZonaZoo lead a sea of red-clad fans in rocking the arena during home games.

The good news: you can still score tickets to some games during the season (try Christmas break, when most students are gone) or, if all else fails, make friends with a season ticket holder. And don't overlook the talented UA women's basketball team, which also plays at McKale Center. The arena is centrally located on the UA campus near several parking garages.

1721 E. Enke Drive
520-621-2211
arizonawildcats.com

TIP
If it's your first time at a Wildcats basketball game, don't sit down too soon—the tradition is for fans to remain standing from the opening tip-off until the visiting team scores its first basket.

HIT THE GREENS
ON A GOLF COURSE

Tucson's year-round sunshine and dry climate draw golfers from around the world. The region's 40-plus courses range from relaxing to championship caliber. (And no, they aren't just one big sand trap—there's plenty of greenery.) Choose among moderately priced—but well-maintained—municipal courses or more expensive and often challenging resort courses, many of which are open to the public.

The top two municipal courses are in the Randolph Golf Complex: **Randolph North**—Tucson's oldest and longest public links at 6,900 yards—and the scenic **Dell Urich** (600 S. Alvernon Way, 520-791-4161). Others are **Silverbell** (3600 N. Silverbell Road, 520-791-5235), **Fred Enke** (8251 E. Irvington Road, 520-791-2539), and **El Rio** (1400 W. Speedway Boulevard, 520-791-4229).

Among the top resort courses are the **Starr Pass Golf Club** (3646 W. Starr Pass Boulevard, 520-791-6270), the **Lodge at Ventana Canyon** (6200 N. Clubhouse Lane, 520-577-4092), and the **Omni Tucson National Golf Resort & Spa** (2727 W. Club Drive, 520-297-2271), site of an annual springtime PGA tourney.

TIP
Reserve tee times at any municipal course at tucsoncitygolf.com. City residents pay about twenty-five percent less than non-residents at public courses.

RIDE ON OVER
TO THE RODEO

Tucson's annual professional rodeo week—known officially as La Fiesta de los Vaqueros—is the time when local dudes and wanna-be cowgals dust off their ten-gallon hats, spit-polish their boots, don their spangled shirts, saddle up their minivans, and head to the rodeo grounds to cheer on the daring steer wrestlers, calf ropers, and barrel racers.

The late February, eight-day celebration of cowboy culture—ninety years and counting—is such a time-honored tradition that Tucson schoolchildren get Rodeo Week off. (Local kids can also compete in their own rodeo events.)

During the week the Tucson Rodeo Parade features a procession of old-time horse-drawn carriages, buggies, and wagons—along with cowboys on horseback, marching bands, and floats—making their way through city streets to the rodeo grounds. It's said to be the world's longest non-motorized parade.

4823 S. 6th Avenue
tucsonrodeo.com
Parade: 520-294-1280, tucsonrodeoparade.org

TIP
From January to March you can also visit
the Tucson Rodeo Parade Museum on the rodeo grounds.
Call 520-294-3636 for information.

CHEER ON THE WOMEN
AT THE ROLLER DERBY

The flamboyant team names alone—Furious Truckstop Waitresses, VICE Squad, Copper Queens, Bandoleras, Saddletramps—are enough to entice a newcomer to this "all girl" sport, as the women of the Tucson Roller Derby describe it. In 2003, local roller skaters helped found the Women's Flat Track Derby Association, and now compete against teams on city, state, and national levels throughout the year.

The action pits "jammers" as they try to skate past their opponents, evading blockers and trying to avoid penalties for grabbing, shoving, and tripping. Competitors are known for tattooed arms, a litany of injuries that only an orthopedist could love, and colorful monikers such as that of the librarian-by-day who skates as "Dewey Decimatrix." Bouts take place about once a month and typically attract raucous crowds to the Tucson Indoor Sports Center; check the website for dates.

1065 W. Grant Road
520-624-1234
tucsonrollerderby.com

CYCLE AROUND
THE OLD PUEBLO

What will it be: a 100-mile-plus bike race or a five-mile fun ride? El Tour de Tucson—billed as "America's Largest Perimeter Bicycling Event"—welcomes riders of all ages and abilities. For one day each November, cyclists wind through and around the city as they compete in races of 104, 75, 55, and 40 miles. Or you can pedal for more modest lengths of eleven, five, or one-quarter miles. El Tour's long-distance races draw top competitors from around the world, while the fun rides draw thousands from around the block.

You'll have plenty of places to practice: the Tucson area offers 600 miles of striped bike paths, 300 miles of mountain biking trails, 200 miles of residential bike routes, and 70 miles of shared routes. The Loop—a paved pathway that encircles most of the city—will eventually total 131 miles.

520-745-2033
perimeterbicycling.com/el-tour-de-tucson

TIP
Another test of speed and endurance—24 Hours in the Old Pueblo (epicrides.com)—pits teams of competing cyclists who pedal for twenty-four straight hours each February; the grueling event attracts 2,000 riders annually.

CHILL OUT
WITH ROADRUNNERS HOCKEY

Hockey in the desert played by a team called the Roadrunners, a bird known for speeding through arid terrain? If that seems odd, look at it this way: cooling off in an icy arena makes perfect sense in the Tucson heat. (Having a fan base supplemented by flocks of Canadian "snowbirds" who spend winters in the city doesn't hurt.) The Roadrunners—the American Hockey League Pacific Division franchise that serves as the top minor league team for the National Hockey League's Phoenix-based Arizona Coyotes—relocated from Massachusetts to Tucson in 2016. The result has been a win-win for Arizona hockey: the wily Coyotes now have a nearby lode of talent to draw upon when needed, while Tucson gets to enjoy one of the world's fastest sports—fitting for a team of Roadrunners.

Tucson Convention Center Arena, 260 S. Church Avenue
866-774-6253
tucsonroadrunners.com

TIP
The Roadrunners' regular season runs from mid-October to mid-April.

SADDLE UP
AT TANQUE VERDE RANCH

If you've ever watched old westerns, you've seen cowboys and outlaws riding horses hell-bent across the saguaro-strewn hills near Tucson. At 650-acre Tanque Verde Ranch—often honored as one of the top family resorts in the country—you can saddle up and steer your mount over some of the same trails (though the hell-bent part is optional).

While Tanque Verde's cattle-ranch roots go back 150 years and its dude-ranch history dates back for a century, today's version features luxury resort amenities like casitas with private patios, tennis courts, a swimming pool, and a spa. But those are mainly for shaking the dust off after a day exploring scenic Saguaro National Park East and environs. The ranch, which keeps 150 horses and still runs a major cattle operation, offers a variety of trail rides, horsemanship lessons, guided biking and hiking trips, and kids' activities.

14301 E. Speedway Boulevard
520-296-6275 or 800-234-3833
tanqueverderanch.com

The Tucson area offers a number of other guest ranches and stables where you can hit the trails on horseback. Here are some of the best:

Once a working cattle ranch, **Rincon Creek Ranch** is now a luxury guest ranch bordering Saguaro National Park East.
14545 E. Rincon Creek Ranch Road, 520-760-5557, rinconcreekranch.com

Luxurious **Hacienda Del Sol Guest Ranch Resort** offers trail rides in the Catalina foothills.
5501 N. Hacienda Del Sol Road, 520-299-1501 or 520-631-3787 (stables), haciendadelsol.com

The **Paniolo Guest Ranch** borders Saguaro National Park West.
6515 W. Ina Road, 520-907-7306, thepanioloranch.com

White Stallion Ranch is a traditional dude ranch, with desert rides.
9251 W. Twin Peaks Road, 520-297-0252, whitestallion.com

Pantano Riding Stables leads trail rides in the desert.
4450 S. Houghton Road, 520-298-8980, horsingaroundarizona.com

Houston's Horseback Riding, run by a rodeo family, offers trail rides and lessons.
12801 E. Speedway Boulevard, 520-298-7450, tucsonhorsebackriding.com

CULTURE AND HISTORY

VISIT EL PRESIDIO,
TUCSON'S BIRTHPLACE

Except for a small chapel situated at the foot of Sentinel Peak ("A" Mountain), the first European structure in Tucson was an adobe fort built in 1775 to protect a Spanish military garrison and settlers from Apache attacks. The northernmost point of the Spanish settlement of Arizona at that time, El Presidio San Augustin Del Tucson featured four 750-foot-long walls up to four feet thick and sixteen feet high, which stood for well over a century before the last section was razed in 1918.

Today much of the eleven acre site north of Congress Street houses government buildings, restaurants, museums, and shops, including some situated in historic nineteenth century structures. The Presidio Museum, located on one corner of the original site, is a reconstruction of the fort and includes an authentic 2,000-year-old Native American pit house that was uncovered by archaeologists.

El Presidio is bounded by Washington, Church, and Pennington Streets and Main Avenue.

Presidio Museum: 196 N. Court Avenue, 520-837-8119, tucsonpresidio.com

TIP

If you walk north from the Tucson Museum of Art and Historic Block along Main Avenue, you'll pass a number of grand homes that once belonged to copper barons and other wealthy merchants. The area was charmingly known as "Snob Hollow."

EXPLORE THE
OLDEST NEIGHBORHOOD

The name *Barrio Viejo* is Spanish for "old neighborhood"—fitting because this is where you'll find the oldest residential area in Tucson that remains largely intact. Most of the city's still-standing nineteenth century Sonoran row houses are located here, many of them restored and serving as residences or offices.

Historic structures include the 1869-era Sonoran-style Cushing Street Bar & Restaurant at the corner of West Cushing Street and South Meyer Avenue and the 1850s-era Camilo House just down the block on South Meyer. Other landmarks are the Teatro Carmen at 380 South Meyer (a onetime Spanish-language theater), and El Tiradito—known as the Wishing Shrine—on South Main Avenue between Cushing and West Simpson Streets. The same block has a small park that once harbored a natural spring and public baths.

tucson.gov

TIP
Situated just south of downtown, the barrio is roughly bounded by
W. Cushing Street on the north, S. Scott Avenue on the east,
W. 18th Street on the south, and I-10 on the west.

FOLLOW A DREAM
TO THE DEGRAZIA GALLERY

When Ted DeGrazia was unable to sell his artworks, he did what every unsung artist would like to do: he built his own galleries to display them. The Tucson artist, who died in 1982, is now well known—his desert landscapes and portraits of Native Americans have hung in major museums—but back in the 1930s and 1940s, when he started work on his complex of Mexican-style adobes in the Catalina Mountain foothills, he labored in anonymity.

Building mostly by hand with the help of friends, he transformed ten acres of cactus-strewn hillside into his own distinctive—and at times eccentric—studio in the sun. DeGrazia's voluminous body of work included hand-crafted jewelry and ceramics as well as paintings, but the gallery complex itself—now a National Historic District—may be his most enduring legacy.

6300 N. Swan Road
520-299-9191
degrazia.org

HONOR THE DEPARTED
AT THE ALL SOULS PROCESSION

Inspired by the Dia de los Muertos—the Mexican Day of the Dead celebration—the annual All Souls Procession has become one of Tucson's most iconic and revered public events. After modest beginnings in 1990, the procession—held in early November each year on or around All Souls Day to honor and mourn the lives of deceased loved ones—now draws some 100,000 participants and spectators.

Mixing the colorful with the macabre, the procession includes giant skull art pieces, the Hungry Ghosts busker troupe, costumed stilt-walkers, acrobats, drummers—and anyone who simply wants to join in. The two-mile route runs from the 6th Avenue underpass to the Mercado San Agustin west of downtown, site of the dramatic finale: a giant urn filled with wishes and messages for the departed is held high in the air and set ablaze.

allsoulsprocession.org

ENCOUNTER ART ON
THE CUTTING EDGE

Tucson has other museums that include contemporary art among their displays, but the Museum of Contemporary Art (MOCA) is the only one for which it is the entire focus. More than twenty years after it opened, MOCA remains on the cutting edge of the art world, staging an eclectic series of exhibitions that test the limits of the creative imagination—and, in some viewers' minds, the concept of what constitutes art itself.

You'll find the works of Tucson artists represented here, along with art pieces from nationally and internationally known painters, sculptors, and other creators of the visual arts. But more importantly to a museum whose stated mission is to "inspire new ways of thinking," MOCA showcases artworks that—whether they delight or disturb our sensibilities—will challenge conventional notions about the intrinsic nature of modern life and aesthetics.

265 S. Church Avenue
520-624-5019
moca-tucson.org

TIP
Admission is free the last Sunday of each month, and free to bicyclists on the second Sunday of each month.

70

SOAR THROUGH THE UNIVERSE
AT THE UA PLANETARIUM

The 43,000-student University of Arizona is one of the main engines driving Tucson's cultural train. A walk around its sunny, pleasant campus will lead you to its oldest building—the centrally located 1891 "Old Main"—past trees and plants from arid and semi-arid regions around the globe (forming an urban arboretum that's the longest continually maintained public green space in the state), and several excellent museums. You can even be transported into deep space.

The star of the Flandrau Science Center and Planetarium is the planetarium's state-of-the-art theater, where 360-degree dome shows whisk you from the ocean depths to the far corners of the universe. The Science Center complex offers hands-on astronomy, geology, and ecology exhibits, as well as the gem-filled UA Mineral Museum, considered one of the finest mineral collections in America.

Cherry Avenue and University Boulevard
520-621-4516
flandrau.org

TIP
For more information about the UA Campus and free walking tours offered during the spring and fall semesters, visit the UA Visitor Center. (811 N. Euclid Avenue, 520-621-5130, arizona.edu/visitor-center)

Arizona State Museum: The region's oldest and largest anthropological museum boasts the world's most comprehensive collection of Southwest Native American pottery and basketry.
1013 E. University Boulevard, 520-621-6302, statemuseum.arizona.edu

Museum of Art: The university's art museum displays eight centuries of eclectic works, including paintings by Jackson Pollock and Georgia O'Keefe.
1031 N. Olive Road, 520-621-7567, artmuseum.arizona.edu

Richard F. Caris Mirror Lab: Guided tours (Monday through Friday) introduce you to the world's largest telescope mirrors—as tall as three-story buildings—and how they're produced.
mirrorlab.as.arizona.edu/tours

TRAVEL TO THE TROPICS
AT BIOSPHERE 2

Where can you go in the Tucson area to encounter a rain forest filled with tropical trees? How about a mangrove swamp—or even a million-gallon mini-ocean? It's all there and more at Biosphere 2, a University of Arizona scientific research, training, and educational facility that replicates exotic world environments in a futuristic desert setting.

Altogether, Biosphere 2 houses seven model ecosystems—most a far cry from Tucson's own landscapes. Working with these models, scientists from several different fields carry out experiments intended to discover how environmental change affects various areas of the planet.

Guided tours take you along indoor–outdoor trails that lead to the rainforest, an ocean-viewing gallery, and other areas. The multi-shaped, mostly glass-covered facilities—which resemble something out of science fiction—are remarkable sights in and of themselves.

32540 S. Biosphere Road, Oracle
520-838-6200
biosphere2.org

TIP
To reach Biosphere 2, drive north from Tucson about twenty-four miles on Oracle Road/Arizona Highway 77.
Turn right onto Biosphere 2 Road at Mile Post 96.5.

DISCOVER DESERT ART
AT TUCSON DART

Opened in 2013, the Tucson Desert Art Museum (Tucson DART) views its mission as helping visitors "visualize history through art." The history is that of the desert Southwest, and the art is a striking collection of textiles, paintings, and artifacts that are attractively displayed in spacious galleries.

Among the museum's prized items are pre-1940s Navajo and Hopi textiles, including chiefs' blankets, saddle blankets, and Yei weavings. Paintings include works by celebrated nineteenth and early twentieth century landscape artists Thomas Moran and Albert Bierstadt, and more contemporary works by Peter Nisbet and the late Howard Post.

Mesoamerican artifacts, photos, maps, and exhibits on Navajo sand painting and early armaments help to further illuminate the cultures of the region. The museum also presents special exhibitions that change each year.

7000 E. Tanque Verde Road
520-202-3888
tucsondart.org

HEAD OUT TO A
HISTORIC SPANISH MISSION

The gleaming Mission San Xavier del Bac, known as the "White Dove of the Desert," is located just south of Tucson on the Tohono O'odham reservation. Occupying an earlier mission site founded by a Spanish priest in 1692, the current church—built from 1783 to 1797 when the land was still part of New Spain—ranks among the finest examples of Spanish Colonial architecture in America. It's also Arizona's oldest standing European structure and a National Historic Landmark.

The mission remains an active church serving the Tohono O'odham people. A museum and video offer historical background, while free docent tours—highlighted by views of original sculptures and painted murals from the 1700s—are offered every morning but Sunday. A gift shop sells Tohono O'odham basketry and other native crafts.

1950 W. San Xavier Road (exit 92 off I-19 south)
520-294-2624
sanxaviermission.org

TIP
The mission offers free admission to visitors from 7 a.m. to 5 p.m. daily except during religious services. Check the website for mass schedules.

SPEND A DAY
IN TOMBSTONE AND BISBEE

Tombstone, Arizona, seventy miles southeast of Tucson, was the legendary site of the famed 1881 Gunfight at the OK Corral—where Wyatt Earp and Doc Holliday battled the Clanton Gang—and of Boothill, where cowboys were buried with their spurs on. On a day trip from Tucson, you can watch reenactments of the gunfight, visit the *Tombstone Epitaph* newspaper office, down a snifter at Big Nose Kate's Saloon, and pay your respects at Boothill. It's part history, part hokum—and on almost everyone's must-do list.

Lesser-known Bisbee, Arizona, another twenty-three miles south of Tombstone, was once the largest town between San Francisco and St. Louis. It's a mile-high, former copper-mining center—and retains its authentic Old West feel while offering up-to-date amenities and mine tours.

Tombstone:
OK Corral: 326 E. Allen Street, 520-457-3456, okcorral.com

Big Nose Kate's Saloon: 421 E. Allen Street, 520 457-3107

Bisbee:
Queen Mine Tour: 520-432-2071, queenminetour.com

Bisbee Mining & Historical Museum: 5 Copper Queen Plaza, 520-432-7071, bisbeemuseum.org

---

TIP
With an early start, you can visit both Tombstone and Bisbee in a day and arrive back in Tucson by sundown—or make a weekend of it.

UNEARTH THE HISTORY
OF "A" MOUNTAIN

Sentinel Peak—which rises on the western edge of downtown across from Tumamoc Hill—acquired its official name back in pioneer days when sentinels posted atop the peak rushed down to warn of an impending Apache attack.

Tucsonans, though, know it better as "A" Mountain. One glance tells you why: the huge "A"—constructed of white-painted rocks that form the University of Arizona logo—that embellishes its eastern side. First constructed in 1915 to celebrate a football victory, the "A" is now repainted annually by university students.

You can drive about two-thirds of the way up Sentinel Peak, park in the lot and walk the rocky trails that lead to the summit for wide-ranging views. You'll be treading the same hillsides inhabited by Native Americans for 4,000 years before the Spanish arrived.

1000 Sentinel Peak Road South
520-791-4873

STEP INTO
SAINT AUGUSTINE CATHEDRAL

One of downtown Tucson's most architecturally distinctive structures, the Saint Augustine Cathedral is best known for its fanciful cast-sandstone façade that depicts various desert plants and animals—saguaros, yuccas, horned toads—as well as a bronze statue of St. Augustine, the city's patron saint.

The Cathedral's current design dates from 1928, when it was transformed from Romanesque Revival into Spanish Colonial Revival style, modeled after a cathedral in northern Mexico. The interior—which displays murals, mosaics, and stained glass windows along the walls and a twelfth century crucifix behind the altar—was rebuilt in 1968, 100 years after completion of the first cathedral on the site.

The Cathedral holds several Roman Catholic masses during the week. The 8 a.m. Spanish-language Sunday mass is especially noteworthy, featuring festive mariachi music.

192 S. Stone Avenue
520-623-6351
cathedral-staugustine.org

TOUR THE
CHILLING TITAN MISSILE MUSEUM

Once a top-secret underground military facility called Complex 571-1, the Titan Missile Museum housed nuclear-armed missiles in the Cold War era. Today it's a sobering reminder of the unthinkable threat of nuclear conflict.

One-hour guided tours visit the launch control center—where a 103-foot-high missile still sits in its launch duct—and take you through a tense simulated launch. The Titan II missile could deliver a nuclear warhead to a target more than 6,000 miles away within a half hour. To activate the missiles, the President would send coded messages to the officers at the site, who would then go through a "fail safe" process of authentication before launch—not knowing what the preprogrammed target would be.

The site, located just fifteen miles south of Tucson, was decommissioned in 1982 and is now a National Historic Landmark.

1580 W. Duval Mine Road, Sahuarita
520-625-7736
titanmissilemuseum.org

ADMIRE THE ARTWORKS
AND ADOBES AT THE ART MUSEUM

The Tucson Museum of Art and Historic Block nicely melds the creations of top global and regional artists with a mix of contemporary and historic architecture. Drawing on its extensive permanent collections as well as temporary exhibitions, the museum's galleries—some situated within pioneer-era adobes—display paintings, drawings, indigenous crafts, and other artworks that range from pre-Columbian to post-modern. Special emphasis is devoted to the art of the American West, Native Americans, and Latin America.

Five nineteenth- and twentieth-century structures stand within or are adjacent to the museum, part of the four-acre Historic Block where Tucson was born in 1775. These include the 1907 Mission Revival-style Corbett House, the mid-nineteenth century La Casa Cordova—Tucson's oldest adobe home—the 1868 (Edward) Fish House, and the mid-1860s Stevens/Duffield houses, which harbor the museum's café.

140 N. Main Avenue
520-624-2333
tucsonmuseumofart.org

TIP
Museum admission is free for all from 5 to 8 p.m. on the first Thursday of every month, and on the second Sunday of each month for local residents.

GET LITERARY
AT THE FESTIVAL OF BOOKS

Mystery fans, cookbook aficionados, sci-fi nerds, poetry fanciers, and political junkies are among the book lovers of all stripes who converge at the annual Tucson Festival of Books, which draws well over 100,000 people a year to the University of Arizona campus for a two-day mid-March celebration of authors and their work.

Since its 2009 debut, the event has blossomed into the third-largest book fest in the country, now attracting up to 400 authors—both big-name and under the radar—who appear in panel discussions, cooking demonstrations, writer workshops, and book signings.

Much of the action takes place outside in big tents on the grassy Mall, where hundreds of exhibitors peddle books, performers entertain, food vendors dispense goodies, and authors gather to meet the public. Admission is free throughout, but many of the popular panel discussions require advance tickets.

tucsonfestivalofbooks.org

TIP
Bring the kids—the Science City tent and other displays geared toward youngsters from toddlers to teens are loaded with interactive activities, storytelling, and costumed characters.

SIZE UP
THE MINI TIME MACHINE

The Mini Time Machine is the legacy of Tucsonan Patricia Arnell, whose lifetime of collecting superb miniature houses and room boxes began as a child, with a single dollhouse. The some 300-piece collection—dating back to the mid-eighteenth century—now occupies more than 10,000 square feet of museum space and is attractively displayed in several uncrowded galleries.

The miniature houses and tableaux depict scenes fanciful and realistic, past and present, near and far. In keeping with the art of fine miniature making, the detail work is often extraordinary, the scale of the tiny figures and objects is precise, and elements of "wonder and whimsy" appear generously throughout. Exhibits range from evocative Christmas and Halloween scenes to antique houses, Edwardian inns, Irish fairy castles, and even dinner parties for dogs—all, of course, in miniature.

4455 E. Camp Lowell Drive
520-881-0606
theminitimemachine.org

TAKE A FLYER
AT THE AIR & SPACE MUSEUM

The Pima Air & Space Museum is so big that, much like some theme parks, it offers two-day tickets as well as single-day passes. Covering some eighty acres and a century of aviation history, it's one of the largest museums of its kind in the world—displaying nearly 300 aircraft both outdoors and within five indoor hangars. Two of the hangars are devoted to World War II planes.

You need at least three or four hours to cover the basics, but you could easily spend more if you have the time and inclination—especially if you take additional tours of the adjacent Aircraft Boneyard, where the U.S. government and military store planes. The museum, though, is a private operation not affiliated with the government or the nearby Davis-Monthan Air Force Base.

6000 E. Valencia Road
520-574-0462
pimaair.org

TIP
Guided walking tours are provided at several of the hangars, but tram tours are available for those who want or need to ride around the sizeable complex.

CELEBRATE PAST AND PRESENT
AT HOTEL CONGRESS

The Hotel Congress is Tucson's most famous lodging, anchoring a prime downtown location since 1919. Over the past century, the Congress has witnessed the city's transition from small town to bustling metropolis, and has played a memorable role in Tucson's colorful history as well: notorious bank robber John Dillinger was captured here in January 1934 when he and his gang—posing under aliases as normal guests—were unmasked by local firemen.

Today, the Congress honors its history by preserving Dillinger-era décor (complete with rotary phones and switchboard) in its forty rooms. But it also keeps up with the current culture with its popular restaurant the Cup Café, its trendy Club Congress bar, and its attractive Copper Hall, scene of special events. The Congress may be a hotel, but for many Tucsonans, it feels like home.

311 E. Congress Street
520-622-8848
hotelcongress.com.

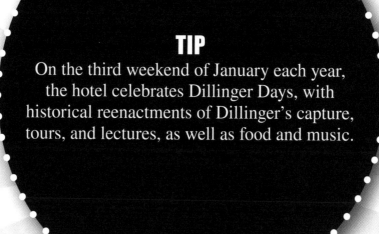

TIP

On the third weekend of January each year, the hotel celebrates Dillinger Days, with historical reenactments of Dillinger's capture, tours, and lectures, as well as food and music.

GAZE UP
AT AN OPEN-AIR ART GALLERY

While Tucson has long been a magnet for muralists, a number of downtown buildings and walls have recently been transformed into an open-air gallery of big, bold, and often fanciful or amusing artworks, thanks in part to a public–private partnership between the City of Tucson Mural Arts Program and the Tucson Arts Brigade with funding from the Tohono O'odham Nation and Visit Tucson. The murals, created by a variety of artists, are as high as seventy feet and as wide as eighty-three feet.

Agave Lady: 440 N. 7th Avenue

Bill Walton Riding a Jackalope: 318 E. Congress Street (by the Rialto Theatre)

Creation Story, Chaos Theory, and Quantum Memory:
213 E. Broadway Boulevard

Greetings from Tucson: 406 N. 6th Avenue (in the alley behind Miller Surplus)

Iconic Tucson: 98 E. Congress Street

Juicy Oranges and Quail: 9 N. Scott Avenue

Latino Culture: 142 E. Pennington Street

Monarch Butterflies, Hummingbirds, and Other Pollinators:
N. 5th Street and E. Toole Avenue

The Jaguar: N. 7th and E. Toole Avenues

Winged Heart: 54 E. Pennington Street

TIP
Herbert Alley off E. Congress Street has changing murals advertising upcoming concerts at the Rialto Theatre.

SHOPPING AND FASHION

BROWSE FOR
BARGAINS AND BLISS
ON 4TH AVENUE

Fourth Avenue between University Boulevard and 8th Street transplants a bit of San Francisco's Haight-Ashbury and New York's Greenwich Village to the city while adding some uniquely Tucson twists. It's a colorful scene blending upscale boutiques with thrift shops, burger joints with designer cafés, tattoo parlors with hair salons, food co-ops with indie bookstores—and just about anything else that falls between the hip, the trendy, and the totally off-the-wall.

It's near the UA campus, so much of its clientele is young (though the eternally youthful hang out here, too). Some of the most intriguing shops are so eclectic they're impossible to categorize—browsing works best. But you may come upon vintage clothing, bronze Buddhas, Mexican rugs, antique furniture, wacky greeting cards, and classic movie posters—sometimes all in the same shop.

www.fourthavenue.org

TIP
Each March and December, 4th Avenue closes to traffic as hundreds of vendors from across the country set up booths at two of Tucson's most popular street fairs. Food trucks and live entertainment add to the merriment.

DRESS LIKE A WILDCAT
IN UA GEAR

One sure sign that you attended the University of Arizona—or wished you'd gone to UA ... or you watch UA games on TV ... or you live in or near Tucson ... or you recently arrived and just want to fit in—is that you're wearing some type of Arizona Wildcat gear.

It could be a red or blue T-shirt or sweatshirt emblazoned with the "A" logo, the snarling face of a wildcat, or simply "Arizona." It could be a baseball cap, basketball jersey, gym shorts, or colorful socks. None of that really matters. The crucial thing is that as soon as you don the gear, you won't be mistaken for a fan of the arch-rival Arizona State Sun Devils. Go Cats!

You can buy official Wildcat gear at the Student Union Memorial Center or at any A-Store branch.

1209 E. University Boulevard
520-621-2426
shop.arizona.edu

TIP

Most Wildcat merchandise is twenty-five percent off at UA Bookstores during "Bear Down Sales" the day before home football games. You can also shop online those days at shop.arizona.edu (using the promo code "beardown").

WANDER IN WONDER
AT OLD TOWN ARTISANS

Care for a sprinkling of history with your shopping experience? At Old Town Artisans, which fills an entire block in the Presidio district—Tucson's oldest neighborhood—you can wander through a half-dozen shops and galleries occupying adobes dating from the 1850s. These are Arizona's longest continuously occupied buildings, with ceilings fashioned from improvised materials: saguaro cactus ribs, packing crates, and whiskey barrel staves.

One shop feeds into the next in a kind of rabbit-warren layout, leading you through a maze of merchandise: custom jewelry, fine art, vintage clothing, mesquite lamps, Native American pottery, vinyl records, local culinary specialties, and quirky gift items galore. After shopping, take a breather in the complex's shady inner courtyard, where there's a restaurant, a pub, and live music.

201 N. Court Avenue, with entrances on Court and Meyer Avenues and
Washington and Telles Streets.
520-622-0351
oldtownartisans.com

GO GOTH OR GLAM
AT HYDRA

Hydra's claim to "setting fashion trends in Arizona since 1994" could well be true—their inventory reads like a catalogue of eclectic, alternative clothing styles of the past two-plus decades. (And maybe some that have yet to appear.) You want retro? They've got retro. You want Goth? They've got Goth. You want zombie? They've got zombie. And a whole lot more: steampunk, burlesque, industrial, NuWave, vintage, vinyl, rockabilly, psychobilly, rock & roll, leather, Western, glam … and just maybe, a leisure suit or two—or not.

And since it stocks both men's and women's wear, including shoes and accessories, Hydra's a one-stop shop for couples off to almost any occasion. As the owners put it, "There's no other boutique like it in Arizona; still isn't." No argument there.

145 E. Congress Street
520-791-3711
hydratucson.com

MINE FOR TREASURES
AT THE GEM SHOW

Tucson's annual Gem, Mineral, & Fossil Showcase is the largest event of its kind on the planet, drawing tens of thousands of bling lovers, rock hounds, and fossil fans for a two-week extravaganza each winter.

Housed in some fifty venues—from hotels to giant tents—the Showcase attracts hundreds of global dealers offering eye-popping displays. Whether you're after a $2 polished agate, a $200,000 necklace, an onyx lamp, or a fossilized dinosaur skeleton, you can find it here. Most shows run from late January to mid-February, just in time to purchase a bauble for Valentine's Day.

It all began modestly in 1955 with the original Gem & Mineral Show, which, over time, spawned the many satellite shows. The original remains the marquee event, filling the Convention Center for four days in mid-February.

Gem, Mineral, & Fossil Showcase: tucsonhows.net
Gem & Mineral Show: Tucson Convention Center, 260 S. Church Avenue, tgms.org/show

---

TIP
Dealers often offer big discounts toward the end of the shows.

FIND YOUR FANCY
AT THE LOST BARRIO SHOPS

Tucson's Lost Barrio isn't actually lost—it's not even missing. And that's all to the good, because a row of some of the city's most intriguing shops await there in plain sight.

The neighborhood, more formally known as Barrio San Antonio, acquired its "Lost" moniker when past highway construction severed it from some adjoining neighborhoods.

You can browse the shops for handcrafted imports, antiques, folk art, custom furniture, fine art, lighting accessories, and more from around the globe.

Rustica (200 S. Park Avenue, 520-623-4435, rusticatucson.com)

Petroglyphs (228 S. Park Avenue, petroglyphstucson.com)

La Casa Mexicana (204 S. Park Avenue, 520-624-1420, lcm-furniture.com)

Colonial Frontiers (244 S. Park Avenue, 520-622-7400; colonialfrontiers.com)

Southwest Furniture & Design (212 S. Park Avenue, 520-461-1341; azsouthwestfurniture.com)

Hollo Collection (208 S. Park Avenue, 520-205-1196, holloantiques.com)

TIP
Access S. Park Avenue from E. Broadway Boulevard near Euclid Avenue, just east of downtown.

PICK UP NATIVE PLANTS
AT DESERT SURVIVORS

The Tucson area has a number of cactus nurseries, but the nonprofit Desert Survivors—which nurtures some 600 plant species native to the Sonoran Desert—has some special qualities. For starters, it's a short drive from downtown, with easy access from north or south just west of highway I-10. The docents there are extremely knowledgeable and can advise you on which plants thrive best in sunshine or in shadow. And all the plants for sale have been cultivated by adults with developmental disabilities, providing much-needed jobs.

You'll find many species of cacti—including barrels, prickly pears, chollas, and saguaros—as well as agaves, grasses, and young palo verde trees. Many plants are conveniently sold in one- or two-gallon pots that can later be transplanted if you wish.

1020 Starr Pass Boulevard
520-791-9309
desertsurvivors.org

HOP ABOARD SUN LINK
FOR DOWNTOWN SHOPPING

The verdict is in: Tucson's recently completed streetcar system – called Sun Link—has played a key role in revitalizing downtown and spurring the growth of shops, restaurants, bars, theaters, residential buildings, and varied businesses along its entire route.

The streetcars wind southwest from the University of Arizona area—home to the 4th Avenue shopping district, Main Gate Square, University bookstores, and other heavily patronized shops—to the Mercado San Agustin public marketplace just west of downtown.

Along the nearly four-mile route, Sun Link cuts through the heart of the city while making a total of twenty-three stops that connect to some 150 shops within easy walking distance. The streetcars run from 7 a.m. to 10 p.m. Monday through Wednesday, 7 a.m. to 2 a.m. Thursday and Friday, 8 a.m. to 2 a.m. Saturday, and 8 a.m. to 8 p.m. Sunday.

520-792-9222
sunlinkstreetcar.com

TIP
You can buy one-day SunGO tickets at any streetcar stop, or download tickets to your smartphone using the GoTucson app.

PULL UP YOUR BOOTS
AT COWBOYS WESTERN WEAR

At some point in Tucson—maybe attending the rodeo, or dancing at a country-western bar, or staying at a dude ranch—you may hanker for some real cowboy duds. If so, head to Cowboys Western Wear—a.k.a. Botas El Mudo—for authentic, high-quality cowboy gear for men, women, and children.

The first thing you notice when you walk into the store is the array of boots in a rainbow of hues—light blue, sage green, reddish brown, shocking pink, canary yellow—and a variety of designs and materials (leather, alligator, ostrich). Choose among many styles and brands, or order a custom-made pair. Then add the pearl snap shirt, the jeans, the leather belt, the brass buckle, the Larry Mahan hat —and your urban cowboy outfit is complete.

1938 S. 6th Avenue
520-882-8383
cowboyswesternwear.net

93

UNLOCK THE SECRETS
OF THE WAREHOUSE ARTS DISTRICT

Tucson's Warehouse Arts District emerged during the 1980s when the state of Arizona bought up blocks of neglected warehouses downtown to make way for a highway. When that plan fell through, the state rented the spaces to artists at low cost, and artists have remained and thrived there ever since—helping to revitalize downtown in the process.

Along E. Toole Avenue and elsewhere in the district, you'll find shared artists' studio spaces, fashion designers, photographers, performance artists, and more. The 1907-era Steinfeld Warehouse (101 W. 6th Street), featuring the Conrad Wilde Gallery, is one prominent exhibition space for artists.

Not all the arts spaces have galleries or retail outlets—you may encounter lots of closed doors—but a stroll around the area can yield some off-the-beaten-track gems, such as the Santa Theresa Tile Works (440 N. 6th Avenue, 520-623-8640), where you can design your own mini-masterpieces made with fanciful tiles.

warehouseartsdistrict.com

TIP
The Warehouse Arts District is bounded roughly by E. Toole Avenue and W. 6th Street west of the railroad tracks and by East 5th Street, N. 4th Avenue, and E. 8th Street to the north and east of the tracks.

121

COUNT ON HIGH QUALITY
AT MUSEUM SHOPS

Some of the most interesting shopping in town can be found within Tucson's museums and botanical gardens. While specific items and emphases vary from shop to shop, these are excellent places to browse for high-quality, authentic jewelry, basketry, pottery, textiles, glasswork, carvings, and crafts—often the work of local and Southwestern artisans as well as those of Native Americans from several tribal nations. You'll also find eclectic selections of regional books and products, as well as children's sections featuring books, toys, and puzzles.

Arizona State Museum
(1013 E. University Boulevard, 520-626-5886, statemuseum.arizona.edu)

Tohono Chul Park
(7366 N. Paseo Del Norte, 520-742-6455, tohonochulpark.org)

Tucson Botanical Gardens
(2150 N. Alvernon Way, 520-326-9686, tucsonbotanical.org)

Tucson Desert Art Museum
(7000 E. Tanque Verde Road, 520-202-3888, tucsondart.org)

Tucson Museum of Art
(140 Main Avenue, 520-624-2333, tucsonmuseumofart.org)

DELVE INTO FINE ART
AT DESERT ARTISANS

A consortium of regional artists and artisans own and operate this jewel of a gallery found in a small shopping center on Tucson's east side. For nearly three decades, the artisans have banded together to cooperatively display and sell their work: exquisite jewelry, stunning glassware, colorful paintings, beautifully crafted ceramics, and intricate basketry. More than sixty local artists contribute, many with their own labeled space in the gallery.

Notable works include clay sculptures of Native Americans by Terry Slonaker, sparkling glass jewelry by Margaret Shirer, and paintings of desert blossoms by Jan Thompson. When you visit the Desert Artisans Gallery, you're likely to meet one of the artists at the front counter; they take turns handling sales duties.

6536 E. Tanque Verde Road (in the La Plaza Shoppes center)
520-722-4412
desertartisansgallery.com

BLOW YOUR OWN
AT SONORAN GLASS

You have two options at the Sonoran Glass School, southern Arizona's top center for all things glass. You can browse the gallery and sculpture garden to shop for glass-art gifts, decorative pieces, and glassware made by faculty, students, and visiting artists—or try your hand (and lung power) at fashioning your own glass creations in the glassblowing studio, choosing your own colors and designs. (Sales benefit the nonprofit school.)

If you wish, you can also watch classes in session; call ahead for the schedule on the day you'd like to visit. If you have a group, ask about the possibility of arranging a guided tour of the facility. Weekend hours at the school are by appointment only.

633 W. 18th Street
520-884-7814
sonoranglass.org

PAY A MOONLIT VISIT
TO METAL ARTS VILLAGE

Housing independent artists and artisans working in a variety of genres—sculpture, painting, custom-designed stained glass, metal works of all kinds, photography, even an award-winning tattoo artist—Metal Arts Village is the creation of attorney-sculptor Stephen Kimble, who designed and built the attractive complex in 2009.

Since these are working studios, not retail operations, buying opportunities from most of the artists are limited to "chance or by appointment"—you might catch one or more on site, but a prior appointment is much safer. Or you can attend one of their Open Studios every month "under the full moon," with all the artists present and live music performed on stage in the Village's attractive sculpture garden. The complex also contains the Tucson Hop Shop, where local craft beers star in an urban beer garden.

3240 N. Dodge Boulevard
520-975-9792
metalartsvillage.com

TIP
One of the studios is occupied by Beads of Courage, a non-profit that donates hand-made beads to children with serious illnesses; each bead commemorates a milestone they have conquered during treatments, helping provide the courage to continue.

TREK ON UP
TO THE NATIONAL PARKS STORE

Even the folks who run Tucson's National Parks Store admit it's off the beaten path, but insist "It's worth the trip!" And they're right. Once there—it's off the highway, miles north of the central city—you'll be rewarded by one of the area's best selections of authentic Native American art, jewelry, and textiles, as well as handmade Mexican crafts. The pottery from Mata Ortiz (a Mexican artists' village) and woven Tarahumara baskets are worth the trip by themselves.

Add to this a superior selection of regional travel and nature books—including a large kids' section focusing on local wildlife—as well as a plethora of park guides, cards, stuffed animals, puzzles, and toys. (Purchases are tax free.) The Parks Store is a beautiful new facility—once you find it.

12880 N. Vistoso Village Drive, Oro Valley
520-622-6014
wnpa.org/national-parks-store

TIP
From downtown Tucson, follow Oracle Road north of Tangerine Road until you reach Rancho Vistoso Road. Turn left and then left again at Innovation Park Drive. Make your final left into Vistoso Park Drive (look for the American flag) and park in the lot. Voilà!

SHOP FARMERS' MARKETS
FOR FRESH FOODS

The Tucson food scene is trending heavily toward fresh foods and local sourcing from organic farms, along with locally crafted specialty items. That should point you straight in the direction of the city's growing array of farmers' markets, which operate year-round (though at different days of the week and times of day).

Heirloom Farmers Markets
(Rillito Park, 4502 N. First Avenue, 520-882-2157, Sundays 9 a.m. to 1 p.m.)

Heirloom Farmers Markets East
(Trail Dust Town, 6541 E. Tanque Verde Road, 520-882-2157, Fridays 9 a.m. to 1 p.m.)

Plaza Palomino Farmers' Market
(Courtyard, 2970 N. Swan Road, 520-327-4676, Saturdays 9 a.m. to 1 p.m. in summer, 10 a.m. to 2 p.m. rest of year)

Rincon Valley Farmers and Artisans Market
(12500 E. Old Spanish Trail, 520-591-2276, Saturdays 8 a.m. to 1 p.m.)

Santa Cruz River Farmers' Market
(Mercado San Agustin, 100 S. Avenida del Convento, 520-882-3304, Thursdays 4 to 7 p.m. in summer, 3 to 6 p.m. rest of year)

Santa Fe Square Farmers Market
(7000 E. Tanque Verde Road, 520-261-6982 Sundays 9 a.m. to 2 p.m.)

ENJOY RELAXED SHOPPING
AT LA ENCANTADA

La Encantada is the most pleasant shopping mall in Tucson. Set in the foothills of the Catalina Mountains overlooking the city, it's an upscale, Spanish-style complex that's user-friendly from start to finish.

First, head for the covered parking—a big plus on intensely hot days. The open-air, bi-level mall, which is pedestrian-only with shaded walkways, is home to mid- to upper-level chains, ranging from Crate & Barrel to Louis Vuitton, with lesser-known specialty stores like Anthropologie and Papyrus in the mix. You'll also find local outlets such as Oils & Olives, which sells the only Arizona-made extra virgin olive oil.

The lower-level courtyard is replete with orange trees, bougainvillea, fountains, and patio tables with chairs. Several good restaurants and lounges offer both indoor and outdoor seating.

2905 E. Sunrise Drive at N. Campbell Avenue
520-276-3800
laencantadashoppingcenter.com

TIP
The Living Room Wine Café & Lounge is a particularly inviting place to relax with food or drink at La Encantada.

SUGGESTED
ITINERARIES

KID FRIENDLY

ONLY IN TUCSON

FREE ACTIVITIES

Set Your Calendar for 2nd Saturdays, 34

Gaze Up at an Open-Air Art Gallery, 108

Explore the Oldest Neighborhood, 88

Head Out to a Historic Spanish Mission, 96

Visit the Dark Side for Starry, Starry Nights, 62

Step into Saint Augustine Cathedral, 99

Honor the Departed at the All Souls Procession, 90

OFF THE BEATEN PATH

Cozy Up to the Bands at 191 Toole, 48

Trek on Up to the National Parks Store, 126

Wander the Desert Gardens of Tohono Chul, 71

Cheer on the Women at the Roller Derby, 79

Make Your Way to the Monterey Court Café, 41

Follow a Dream to the DeGrazia Gallery, 89

Blow Your Own at Sonoran Glass, 124

Pay a Moonlit Visit to Metal Arts Village, 125

Pull Up Your Boots at Cowboys Western Wear, 120

ACTIVITIES
BY SEASON

Much of Tucson takes the summer off—or takes off for the summer—because of the often intense heat. Be advised that strenuous outdoor activity—such as hiking—can be dangerous in summer. (Carry lots of water, wear sun protection, and let someone know your plans.) In general, winter is Tucson's busiest season, but many activities take place October through April, and most attractions stay open year-round—sometimes with shorter hours.

WINTER

4th Avenue street fairs, 112

24 Hours in the Old Pueblo bike race, 80

A Tucson Pastorela (Borderlands Theater), 55

Arizona Wildcat basketball, 76

Desert Song Festival, 52

Dillinger Days at the Hotel Congress, 107

Gem and Jam Fest, 53

Gem & Mineral Show, 116

Gem, Mineral, and Fossil Showcase, 116

Handel's *Messiah* (Tucson Symphony Chorus), 35

Holiday Nights at Tohono Chul, 71

Roadrunners hockey, 81

Rodeo and Rodeo Parade, 78

The *Nutcracker* (Ballet Tucson), 51

Tucson Craft Beer Crawl, 6

Tucson Jazz Festival, 53

SPRING

SUMMER

FALL

INDEX